# Crochet Colorwork
## *Made Easy*

### Simple Techniques
to Create Multicolor
Sweaters, Accessories
and Home Decor

~

## Claire Goodale
Creator of E'Claire Makery

PAGE STREET
PUBLISHING CO.

PAGE STREET
PUBLISHING CO.

First published in 2021 by

Page Street Publishing Co.

27 Congress Street, Suite 105

Salem, MA 01970

www.pagestreetpublishing.com

Distributed by Macmillan, sales in Canada by The Canadian Manda Group.

25  24  23  22  21      1  2  3  4  5

ISBN-13: 978-1-64567-376-7

ISBN-10: 1-64567-376-6

Library of Congress Control Number: 2021930228

Cover and book design by Laura Benton for Page Street Publishing Co.

Photography by Megan Helm Photography

Printed and bound in China

# Crochet Colorwork
## Made Easy

**To Stephen,**
who has never lost faith that my dreams can come true

# Contents

# Introduction

Hello, maker!

Welcome to the wonderful world of crochet colorwork! I am so excited to open the door for you into an amazing aspect of crochet that has endless possibilities for what you can create. From beautiful garments that feature intricate colorwork to hats, blankets, shawls and more, you'll be able to create projects that combine beauty and functionality. Colorwork isn't just for knitters; it's for crocheters, too!

My crochet journey started on a couch at my grandparents' house on a cold winter night when I was seven years old. My grandma was determined for the grandkids to learn how to crochet, so she sat us all down and taught us how to do the chain stitch. As soon as I started working with the yarn, I was hooked! That launched me into begging my mom to buy me some crochet books so that I could learn how to do it better. I quickly fell in love with all different types of crochet, and I pursued my dream of being a crochet designer in 2018 when I started my business, E'Claire Makery.

As I began designing different patterns for my business, I felt like something was missing in my designs. I tried to be like other designers I saw, but I couldn't pinpoint the tiny little puzzle piece that I was missing. While I was searching, I kept looking at all of the beautiful knitted colorwork sweaters, wishing that I could somehow do them. Then, I discovered tapestry crochet. That changed everything. I couldn't believe that I could create pictures with yarn! I dove headfirst into the wondrous world of colorwork and learned how to do intarsia crochet and fair isle crochet, too.

While falling in love with crochet colorwork, being the overachiever that I am, I set out to design my own patterns. I wanted to bring gorgeous knitted colorwork designs to crochet, especially when it came to garments. Colorwork garments are often not made for all sizes, so I make it a priority in my designs to create colorwork garments that span a wide variety of them. All of the designs in this book are size inclusive and will look beautiful on you.

I fell in love with crochet colorwork, and now it is my main goal in life to help others discover it, too! Colorwork isn't a scary, unreachable thing. You can do it! In this book, I will teach you all the things you'll need to know to get started with colorwork. Think of me as your colorwork tour guide, who will be with you each step of the way through your journey. There are lots of tutorials and beginner patterns so that you can create the beautiful colorwork projects you've been dreaming of.

I hope you fall in love with colorwork!

*Claire A. Goodale*

# An Intro to Colorwork Crochet

## What Is Crochet Colorwork?

Now that you are ready to set forth into the world of crochet colorwork, you might be wondering, what exactly is it? Crochet colorwork is the technique by which we can create pixelated designs, pictures and patterns using different colors of yarn. With it you can capture all of the beautiful colorwork designs that you see in knitting. It centers around three main techniques: tapestry crochet, intarsia crochet and fair isle crochet. It can also be used in Tunisian crochet and corner to corner crochet, but in this book we'll be focusing on the three main techniques.

If you haven't done any of these techniques, then they might seem intimidating because they sound completely different than normal crochet. Guess what? All three techniques use the crochet stitches you are used to using! They each have special ways that they use basic crochet techniques, with the main difference lying in how they carry yarn. Let's dive into what each technique means!

**Tapestry Crochet:** Tapestry crochet is the colorwork method that creates a fabric with a woven appearance. Often this term is used to encompass the entirety of crochet colorwork; however, it is a separate technique from the others with its own distinct characteristics. The main difference is that it involves carrying the unused colors of yarn as you crochet each stitch. (It is usually done with two colors in the whole project or row, so you only carry one color as you work with the other.) Since you carry the yarn, the colors sometimes peek through the stitches, which gives it the woven look. It also creates a reversible project since the yarn is carried throughout.

**Intarsia Crochet:** This technique is the colorwork method that really opens up the world of designs and colors that you can use in crochet. You can use any number of colors you want, and you don't carry the unused colors. Instead, you create bobbins (little balls of yarn to use) that you attach at the different points as you need them. If you are crocheting a detailed colorwork pattern, this is the best method to use so that your fabric doesn't get too thick from so many colors. It truly allows you to create artwork with yarn!

**Fair Isle Crochet:** This colorwork technique is the one that looks the most like stranded knitting. Often the definition is based on using the waistcoat stitch that looks like a stockinette stitch in knitting. However, if you compare it side by side with the fair isle knitting technique, the fair isle technique is centered around the way that the yarn is carried as well as the design style. Similar to tapestry crochet, you only use two colors per row, but what sets it apart is that instead of carrying the yarn through each stitch, you use something called floats. Floats are small strands of yarn that stretch across the back of your work, which we'll discuss in depth in the fair isle chapter of this book (page 111). The designs of fair isle crochet also mimic the designs of fair isle knitting that are derived from the Fair Isle. This detailed and densely patterned design style can also be used in crochet!

## How to Put Colors Together

One of the biggest questions I get when I create a design is, "How do I put colors together?" Sometimes, the fear of not being able to put colors together will stop someone from jumping into crochet colorwork. Want to know a secret? Anyone can put colors together! My favorite part about colorwork is putting together color palettes, and with a few simple steps, you can, too!

**Step 1:** What colors go together? When it comes to putting colors together, it really helps to create a firm foundation that you can build your color palettes around. Most colors are grouped into three separate categories: warm, cool and neutral. Warm colors include reds, oranges and yellows. Cool colors include blues, greens and purples. Then neutral colors include black, brown, white and gray.

Often the best types of color palettes are those within the same family, but one of my favorite parts of putting colors together is mixing and matching color families to blend together. You can easily pair warm and cool colors with ones in the neutral color category, which leads to some amazing color possibilities! You can see this reflected in a lot of the patterns in this book. Orange looks great with a neutral like tan or white, and green pairs well with a silvery gray. You can even pair yellow and purple together if you have the right shades!

If you need some help with knowing what colors go together, take a look at the color wheel included in this section, and have fun mixing and matching different tones. The best part about choosing colors is that it is totally up to you how you want to customize your project!

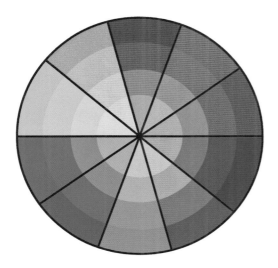

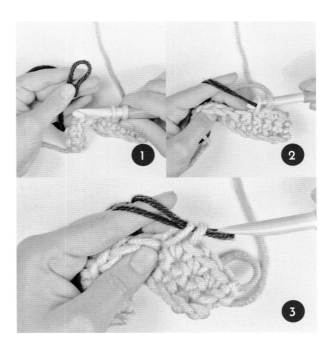

**Step 2:** Choosing your color palette. Whenever I pick out the colors that I will be using for my designs, I always start with a color to center the rest of my choices around. This is usually the main color of the design. Then, when I am adding more colors, I'll experiment with seeing what other colors go well with the main one. When I'm picking these all out, I usually have a theme or feel that I am trying to reflect in the yarn. For example, the Trailhead Ruana on page 103 was built around the feel of a hike in the woods. I started with taupe as the main color to capture the stone and earth of the mountains. Then I picked out accent colors that would capture the woodsy feel that I was going for: colors like orange, green and mustard. They all have a similar rustic hue, which helps them all blend together.

When it comes to pairing colors together with yarn, one of the best tips I have is to pick out colors within the same yarn line! Yarn companies design their yarn lines to be paired together, giving them complementary tones. If you aren't ready to get adventurous with color yet, picking one yarn line to use is a great place to start.

## Basic Colorwork Techniques

### Changing Colors

The first technique that you'll need to know how to do properly is changing colors as you crochet. With this simple technique, you'll be able to have seamless color changes that really pop! To change colors, perform the following steps:

### Changing Colors on the Right Side

**Step 1:** When you are ready to change colors, take the yarn you will be using next.

**Step 2:** On the last yarn over where you complete the stitch, yarn over with your new color of yarn instead of the color you've been using.

**Step 3:** Pull the yarn through the rest of the loops of the stitch, and you'll now be able to use the new color. You can use this technique to change colors every time you need to switch on the right side.

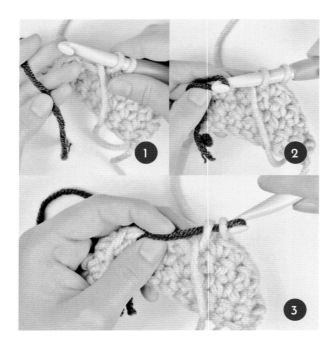

## Changing Colors on the Wrong Side

**Step 1:** When you are about to change to a new color, take the yarn you will be using next.

**Step 2:** On the last yarn over where you complete the stitch, yarn under instead of the yarn over you normally do. Yarning under on the wrong side of your work helps the color transitions to be smoother and the yarn won't pop out as much.

**Step 3:** Pull the yarn through the rest of the loops of the stitch, and you'll now be able to use the new color. You can use this technique to change colors every time you need to switch on the wrong side.

## Adjusting Tension

Having proper tension is crucial to crochet colorwork! If your tension is too tight, your projects will bunch up, and if your tension is too loose then you will have big holes where you've switched colors. When you have just the right tension, your projects won't have any holes and zero bunching! Here are some of my tips for achieving proper tension with crochet colorwork:

**Step 1:** To prevent holes in your work when you switch colors, you'll want to do this simple trick. When you are changing colors, instead of moving on to the next stitch right away, make sure that you pull on the yarn that you switched from. Pull the yarn until the stitch tightens up and isn't loose, but not to the point where the stitch is too tight and the loops start to disappear.

**Step 2:** If you are carrying your yarn when using the tapestry (page 23) or fair isle crochet (page 111) techniques, this simple tip will prevent bunching. Hold the yarn you are carrying in the back of the work, but don't pull it tight. Holding it looser will ensure that when you switch back to the color you're carrying, the back of your work won't be so tight that the fabric can't bend. You can also stretch the work you've already done to double check if the yarn is too tight.

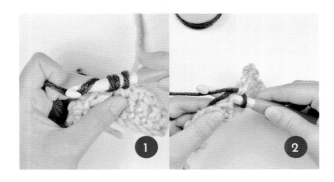

## Weaving in Ends

A common reason I often hear why people don't do colorwork is that they are afraid of all of the ends to weave in. Well, what if I told you that there are a few secrets to have fewer ends? It's true! I do the following crochet tips and have virtually no ends to weave in when I'm done with my project.

**Step 1:** Use an end to do a stitch. This is one of my most-used tricks. Whenever I join a new color to a project, I will leave an end that is long enough to do one stitch. As I do the next stitch, I double up the yarn, using the new yarn strand as well as the end of the old one. That helps secure the end within your project, and then you just have to trim what is left over to have it woven in. It works so well!

**Step 2:** Carry the end. Another frequently used technique is to carry the end from the yarn you joined across the back of your stitches. As I do the next few stitches after joining the new color, I will carry the end across the back of those stitches to weave it in. This helps secure the yarn to the back of your work, and you are able to weave in as you go.

## How to Read a Chart

Charts are one of the parts of crochet colorwork that change the whole game! You can use a simple graph to create crochet magic. If you've never used a chart before, I'm here to help! There are a few different things that you'll need to know in order to use them for your crochet projects. Each design in this book includes a chart for the colorwork to help make it a lot easier. Here are all of the things you need to know to use charts:

### Types of charts

In this book, there are a few different types of charts that I use for the patterns. There are ones that are squares, which are used for designs made with panels or ones that don't include increases. There are also ones that include increases and are shaped more like triangles.

### Reading the chart

When reading the chart, each square on the chart counts as one stitch. Colorwork charts are different than traditional charts that use symbols on a graph to indicate what you need to do. Instead, colorwork charts use filled-in squares to let you know what color you need for each stitch, with the type of stitch used for the whole pattern staying the same. The rows are read starting from either left or right across to the other side, and alternate between reading it back and forth. The most common directions are: alternating right to left, alternating left to right or from the right to left for each row. Depending on the pattern, the chart will also be read starting from top down or from the bottom up. Use the sequence of numbers along the edges of the chart to help guide you.

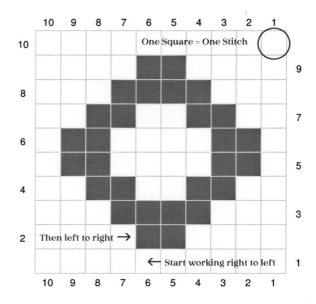

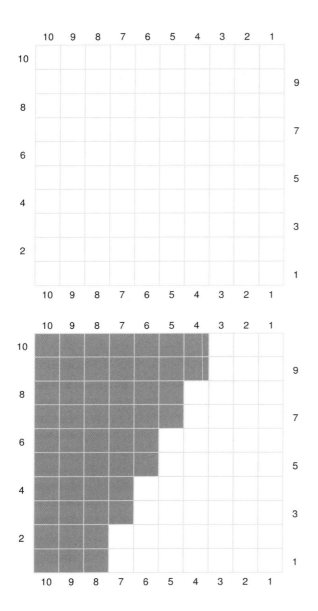

## No increases vs. increases

When a chart does not include increases within the colorwork, it will be a square that shows the complete portion of the colorwork that you do. If a chart does include increases, then it will start with a small number and slowly increase outward to the left. There will be gray space on the left side that indicates where no stitches are, and will have the stitches you work colored in. When there is an increase on a row on the chart, there will be one more colored stitch added in on the right. The last two stitches on the left are the stitches used in the increase. Sometimes the stitches will be two different colors, which means that you'll do a stitch of each color in that stitch.

Here are some notes that you will need for reading the charts in this book:

- Each square on the chart counts as one stitch. Whether you're using single crochet, half double crochet or another stitch, when doing colorwork, a square on a chart counts as a single stitch.

- When a square is a different color than the previous one, that indicates that you will be changing colors on the last yarn over to the color you'll use for the next square.

- Within each pattern, it will indicate the correct direction in which to read the chart. For most of the patterns in this book, the charts are read starting at the bottom and going up to the top. They also are read from right to left, and alternating between that and left to right on the next row. If a chart for a certain pattern differs from this, then the pattern will indicate that.

# General Notes for All Patterns

## Pattern Notes

- All patterns use US crochet terminology.

- Each chain stitch at the beginning of a row/round does not count in the final stitch count for the row/round throughout each pattern.

- I recommend reading through each pattern completely to make sure that you understand each step of what you'll be doing before you begin.

- Color changes happen in the middle of the rows or rounds of each pattern. The color changes are indicated in the written pattern by a new color in parentheses (for example: (MC) sc 1, (CC) sc 2).

## Pattern Difficulty Levels

**Beginner:** Expands basic crochet techniques by using simple stitch patterns and colorwork. Includes little to no shaping.

**Intermediate:** Projects with a little more of a challenge, such as using more colors for colorwork, or using shaping for patterns.

**Advanced:** Complex projects using a variety of techniques and more detailed colorwork designs.

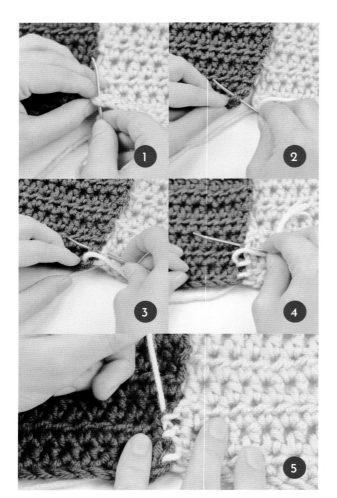

# Seaming Crochet Pieces Together

Sometimes the idea of seaming crochet pieces together can seem very intimidating; however, I believe that it all comes down to just finding the right method that works for you. There are a few different methods here that you can use for seaming crochet pieces together, as well as my favorite way to seam items in the round.

## Whip Stitch

**Step 1:** Thread the needle and turn the crochet pieces wrong-side up. Insert the needle through the corner on the right side and pull the yarn through.

**Step 2:** Insert the needle through the bottom corner on the left side, and pull through.

**Step 3:** Move the needle back to the right side and insert it horizontally through a stitch on the right side through to one on the left.

**Step 4:** Keep doing step 3 all the way up the rest of the edges to create stitch bars that go from one side to the other.

**Step 5:** As you go, you can pull the yarn every five or so stitches to tighten up the seam and secure the two pieces together. Finally fasten off and weave in the ends.

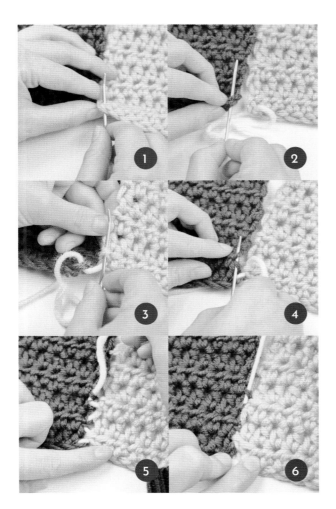

## Mattress Stitch

**Step 1:** Thread the needle and turn the crochet pieces right-sides out. Insert the needle up through the bottom right corner and back up vertically through the next stitch on the right side.

**Step 2:** Move the needle over to the left side, and go up through the left corner and back up vertically through the next stitch on the left side.

**Step 3:** Go back over to the right side and repeat step 1.

**Step 4:** Then move back over to the left side, and repeat step 2.

**Step 5:** As you keep repeating steps 1 and 2 all the way up the pieces, you'll be creating little Vs.

**Step 6:** Every five or so stitches, pull the yarn to tighten the stitches and secure the two pieces together. Finally fasten off and weave in the ends.

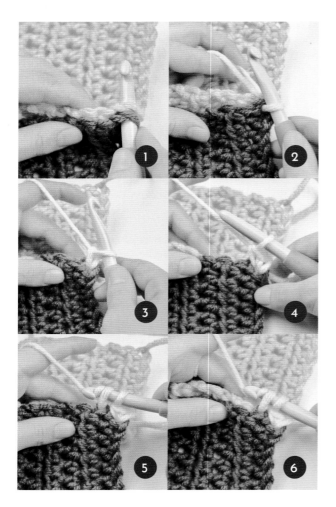

## Single Crochet Seam

**Step 1:** Take your crochet hook and the yarn you'll be using for seaming the two pieces together. With right sides together, insert the hook through the bottom two corners of both pieces.

**Step 2:** Slip stitch yarn through the corners to pull up a loop.

**Step 3:** Once you've done that, chain 1.

**Step 4:** Single crochet 1 through the corners that you slip stitched through.

**Step 5:** Single crochet 1 through both pieces in the next stitch along the edge.

**Step 6:** Keep repeating step 5 until you have finished single crocheting along both edges. Finally fasten off and weave in the ends.

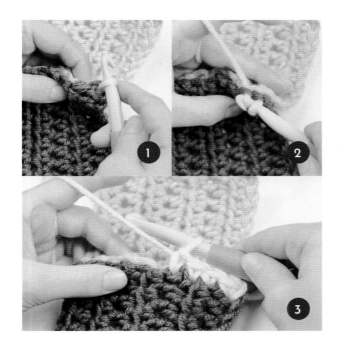

## Slip Stitch Seam

**Step 1:** With the right sides of the crochet pieces together, insert the hook through the bottom corners and slip stitch through both corners.

**Step 2:** Insert the hook into the next stitch through both pieces and slip stitch through them.

**Step 3:** Keep repeating step 2 until you've gone all the way along the edges of both pieces. Finally fasten off and weave in the ends.

## Basting Stitch for Projects in the Round

**Step 1:** Start by threading your needle and inserting it up through one of the stitches of the top where you are closing.

**Step 2:** Skipping one to two stitches, insert the needle back down through a stitch (see photo 2). Skip one to two more stitches, and insert the needle back up through a stitch.

**Step 3:** Repeat step 2 all the way around the part you are closing, pulling the yarn as you go to tighten it.

**Step 4:** Once you are done sewing around the top, pull the yarn until the top is closed all the way. Finally fasten off and weave in the ends.

# Tapestry Crochet

**If you are new to crochet colorwork,** tapestry crochet is the perfect starting point for beginners. It is the easiest combination of crochet techniques you already know, along with just the right amount of adding in a few splashes of color. If you've been dreaming of knitted colorwork patterns, but don't knit, then tapestry crochet will help you make those dreams come true.

Tapestry crochet gets its name from the beautiful woven tapestries that it is able to mimic by creating a woven fabric with yarn. Often tapestry crochet is a term that is mistakenly used to describe any type of crochet colorwork. This technique, however, specifically refers to using just two colors of yarn that are carried throughout the entire design. This adds a unique texture, as hints of the color you aren't using peek through the stitches. By carrying the yarn, you can also create a reversible fabric—since the yarn is within the stitches and helps the overall design be the same on both sides. With the tapestry crochet technique, you'll use two colors to create dynamic pixelated designs, ranging from geometric shapes to floral accents and more!

When it comes to crochet colorwork, tapestry crochet will always be my first love. It combines knitted colorwork, cross stitch and crochet all into one technique. You can take any knitted chart, pixelated drawing, cross stitch pattern or graph and bring it to life using tapestry crochet!

You might be wondering, what other benefits does tapestry crochet have to offer? Two of the most common fears I hear from people about why they do not want to do colorwork are that they are scared of all the ends to weave in or that they are afraid of the different yarns tangling together. Since you are just using two colors and carry the yarn throughout the pattern, managing the yarn is a lot easier. You'll only have two ends to weave in, and I'll be showing you a trick for how to do it as you go. I'll also show you how to prevent your yarn from tangling! Soon those worries you had about colorwork will disappear, and you'll be ready to dive into the more complex techniques like intarsia (page 75) and fair isle crochet (page 111).

In this chapter, I'll be walking you through how to do tapestry crochet and sharing all of the tips for it that I've learned along the way. From how to carry yarn to reading the graphs, I'll teach you each step for this technique. You'll also find patterns I've created that are perfect for beginners, like the Diamond Reflections Pillow (page 27) and the Desert Diamonds Top (page 46)! Let me tell you, once you start doing tapestry crochet, you won't want to stop!

## How to Do Tapestry Crochet Worked Flat and in the Round

When it comes to any type of crochet colorwork, there are a few differences you'll find when working it flat in a panel versus in the round. When you work it flat, you'll have a right and wrong side, and when doing it in the round, you often work on just the right side. Here are some tips for working flat and in the round:

# Basic Tapestry Crochet Techniques

### How to Carry Yarn

With tapestry crochet, the main technique you'll need to know is how to carry yarn. You'll carry your yarn whenever you aren't using the unused color of yarn in your project to the point that you will need it. To carry your yarn, follow the steps below.

**Step 1** (photo 1): Start by taking the unused color and holding it along the back of your work at the top of the stitches.

**Step 2** (photo 2): As you start your next stitch, insert your hook into the next stitch. Pull your yarn over around the unused yarn and through the stitch, securing it along the top.

**Step 3** (photo 3): Until you use the unused color again, repeat step 2, which will carry your yarn along the stitches until it is needed.

## Working Flat

*   **Carrying yarn:** When you work flat, you will be switching back and forth between the right and wrong sides, and you will always carry the yarn on the wrong side. When you work on the right side, you'll carry the yarn on the wrong side of the work (the side facing away from you) and keep all of your yarn strands on that side (see photo 1). When you work on the wrong side, you'll still carry the yarn on the wrong side, but it will be facing you this time (see photo 2). This helps the front of your project stay cohesive and come out cleaner.

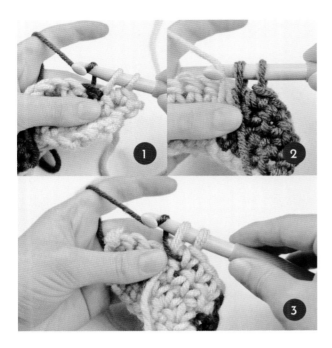

- **Switching colors:** When you are changing colors in tapestry crochet, you'll want to yarn over the yarn color you're switching to on the right side (see photo 1 above) and yarn under when you are changing on the wrong side (see photo 2). If you want your color changes to look cleaner, I recommend not carrying the yarn on the last stitch before you switch colors (see photo 3). When you change colors, the yarn you have been carrying will often poke through when you switch colors, which changes the look of the previous stitch. If you don't carry the yarn on that last stitch, then it won't poke through and the stitch will look solid instead of multicolored.

## Working in the Round

- **Carrying yarn:** When you work in the round, you'll mainly be working on the right side. You'll always carry the yarn on the back of the work (see photo 1), unless the pattern you're doing has you turn each round. The tapestry crochet patterns worked in the round for this book are always worked on the right side. Essentially, you carry the yarn continuously in the round, even over the chain stitches at the beginning (see photo 2).

- **Switching colors:** Since it is mainly worked on the right side (see photo 1), you will always do yarn overs (not yarn unders) when you change colors.

- **Offsetting slanting of stitches:** When you crochet in the round, the stitches will often have a slight slant to them. This is especially noticeable in the round. To fix that problem, the stitches are modified to work in the back loops only (see photo 1 above). This helps straighten out the stitches and allows the colorwork to sit on itself better. This technique is taught in the Queen of Diamonds Hat (page 32).

## How to Prevent Yarn from Tangling

I've got a trick that will help you prevent pesky tangles in your tapestry crochet.

### When working on the right side:

**Step 1:** When you start your project, choose a side that you are going to keep each color on. Since we use two colors for tapestry crochet, I assign one color to the left and one to the right. For the rest of the project, the yarn will stay on its respective side. Do not cross them over each other!

**Step 2:** When you get to a color change, if you are switching to the left color, instead of doing a yarn over to switch colors, do a yarn under underneath the left color. You'll go underneath the new color, which helps you prevent crossing the colors over each other.

**Step 3:** If you are using the color on the right, do a yarn over, making sure to keep the right color on the right side. By doing a yarn over for the right color, you'll prevent the yarn from getting tangled with the left one.

**When working on the wrong side (see photo 4):** Note, if you are working on the wrong side, it will differ slightly from the right side of your project. You will do a yarn under for both colors, but keep them on separate sides.

*Inspired by geometric tile designs, the Diamond Reflections Pillow is a modern and boho tapestry crochet pillow perfect for beginners. Its simple, stylish design brings a modern flair to the tapestry crochet technique that will get you hooked on it. With this straightforward pillow made from two panels sewn together, you'll be able to put all of the tapestry crochet basics into practice: from reading charts to carrying your yarn throughout the pattern.*

# Diamond Reflections Pillow

## Pattern Level: Beginner

**Gauge:** 4" x 4" (10 x 10 cm) square = 9 hdc x 7 rows

**Dimensions:** 16" x 16" (41 x 41 cm) (fits a 16" x 16" [41 x 41-cm] pillow form)

**Hook:** US L/11 8mm

**Yarn:** Lion Brand Color Made Easy (Yarn Weight 5 Bulky, 247 yds [226 m], 7 oz [200 g], 100 percent acrylic) in two colors:
- Millennial Pink (CC)
- Pomegranate (MC)

**Approximate Yarn Yardage:**
MC = 247 yds (226 m)
CC = 247 yds (226 m)

**Extra Materials:**
Yarn needle

**Abbreviations:**
ch = chain
st(s) = stitch(es)
hdc = half double crochet
MC = main color
CC = contrast color
yo = yarn over

# Diamond Reflections Pillow (Continued)

## Chart

Main Color

Contrast Color

For chart notes and how to read a chart, see pages 15-17.

## Pillow Panel (Make 2)

You can use the chart on this page to complete the pattern or the written version of the pattern below.

(MC) ch 38.

**Row 1:** Starting from third ch from hook, hdc 36. On the last st of this row, switch to CC by using CC for the final yo. [36 sts]

Starting with the next row, we will be starting to add in the colorwork. I recommend placing stitch markers at each of the points where you will switch colors. This helps make sure you have the right count for each of the stitch colors!

**Row 2:** (CC) ch 2 (does not count as a stitch throughout), turn, hdc 2, (MC) hdc 4, (CC) hdc 3, (MC) hdc 4, (CC) hdc 3, (MC) hdc 4, (CC) hdc 3, (MC) hdc 4, (CC) hdc 3, (MC) hdc 4, (CC) hdc 2. [36 sts]

**Row 3:** (MC) ch 2, turn, hdc 1, (CC) hdc 2, (MC) hdc 2, (CC) hdc 2, (MC) hdc 1, (CC) hdc 2, (MC) hdc 2, (CC) hdc 2, (MC) hdc 1, (CC) hdc 2, (MC) hdc 2, (CC) hdc 2, (MC) hdc 1, (CC) hdc 2, (MC) hdc 2, (CC) hdc 2, (MC) hdc 1, (CC) hdc 2, (MC) hdc 2, (CC) hdc 2, (MC) hdc 1. [36 sts]

**Row 4:** (MC) ch 2, turn, hdc 2, (CC) hdc 4, (MC) hdc 3, (CC) hdc 4, (MC) hdc 3, (CC) hdc 4, (MC) hdc 3, (CC) hdc 4, (MC) hdc 2. [36 sts]

# Diamond Reflections Pillow (Continued)

**Row 5:** (MC) ch 2, turn, hdc 3, (CC) hdc 2, (MC) hdc 5, (CC) hdc 2, (MC) hdc 5, (CC) hdc 2, (MC) hdc 5, (CC) hdc 2, (MC) hdc 5, (CC) hdc 2, (MC) hdc 3. [36 sts]

**Row 6:** (MC) ch 2, turn, hdc 6, (CC) hdc 3, (MC) hdc 18, (CC) hdc 3, (MC) hdc 6. [36 sts]

**Row 7:** (MC) ch 2, turn, hdc 5, (CC) hdc 2, (MC) hdc 1, (CC) hdc 2, (MC) hdc 6, (CC) hdc 4, (MC) hdc 6, (CC) hdc 2, (MC) hdc 1, (CC) hdc 2, (MC) hdc 5. [36 sts]

**Row 8:** (MC) ch 2, turn, hdc 4, (CC) hdc 2, (MC) hdc 3, (CC) hdc 2, (MC) hdc 4, (CC) hdc 6, (MC) hdc 4, (CC) hdc 2, (MC) hdc 3, (CC) hdc 2, (MC) hdc 4. [36 sts]

**Row 9:** (MC) ch 2, turn, hdc 5, (CC) hdc 2, (MC) hdc 1, (CC) hdc 2, (MC) hdc 4, (CC) hdc 3, (MC) hdc 2, (CC) hdc 3, (MC) hdc 4, (CC) hdc 2, (MC) hdc 1, (CC) hdc 2, (MC) hdc 5. [36 sts]

**Row 10:** (MC) ch 2, turn, hdc 6, (CC) hdc 3, (MC) hdc 4, (CC) hdc 3, (MC) hdc 4, (CC) hdc 3, (MC) hdc 4, (CC) hdc 3, (MC) hdc 6, on the last yo of the last st, switch the CC for a smoother color transition. [36 sts]

> **Pro Tip**
>
> If the first stitch in the next row starts with a different color than you end the row with, finish off the last stitch of the row by switching to the color you'll need during the last yo.

**Row 11:** (CC) ch 2, turn, hdc 1, (MC) hdc 11, (CC) hdc 3, (MC) hdc 6, (CC) hdc 3, (MC) hdc 11, (CC) hdc 1. [36 sts]

**Row 12:** (CC) ch 2, turn, hdc 2, (MC) hdc 9, (CC) hdc 3, (MC) hdc 8, (CC) hdc 3, (MC) hdc 9, (CC) hdc 2. [36 sts]

**Row 13:** (MC) ch 2, turn, hdc 1, (CC) hdc 2, (MC) hdc 7, (CC) hdc 3, (MC) hdc 4, (CC) hdc 2, (MC) hdc 4, (CC) hdc 3, (MC) hdc 7, (CC) hdc 2, (MC) hdc 1. [36 sts]

**Row 14:** (MC) ch 2, turn, hdc 2, (CC) hdc 2, (MC) hdc 5, (CC) hdc 3, (MC) hdc 4, (CC) hdc 4, (MC) hdc 4, (CC) hdc 3, (MC) hdc 5, (CC) hdc 2, (MC) hdc 2. [36 sts]

**Row 15:** (MC) ch 2, turn, hdc 3, (CC) hdc 2, (MC) hdc 3, (CC) hdc 3, (MC) hdc 4, (CC) hdc 2, (MC) hdc 2, (CC) hdc 2, (MC) hdc 4, (CC) hdc 3, (MC) hdc 3, (CC) hdc 2, (MC) hdc 3. [36 sts]

**Row 16:** (MC) ch 2, turn, hdc 3, (CC) hdc 2, (MC) hdc 3, (CC) hdc 3, (MC) hdc 4, (CC) hdc 2, (MC) hdc 2, (CC) hdc 2, (MC) hdc 4, (CC) hdc 3, (MC) hdc 3, (CC) hdc 2, (MC) hdc 3. [36 sts]

**Row 17:** (MC) ch 2, turn, hdc 2, (CC) hdc 2, (MC) hdc 5, (CC) hdc 3, (MC) hdc 4, (CC) hdc 4, (MC) hdc 4, (CC) hdc 3, (MC) hdc 5, (CC) hdc 2, (MC) hdc 2. [36 sts]

**Row 18:** (MC) ch 2, turn, hdc 1, (CC) hdc 2, (MC) hdc 7, (CC) hdc 3, (MC) hdc 4, (CC) hdc 2, (MC) hdc 4, (CC) hdc 3, (MC) hdc 7, (CC) hdc 2, (MC) hdc 1. [36 sts]

**Row 19:** (CC) ch 2, turn, hdc 2, (MC) hdc 9, (CC) hdc 3, (MC) hdc 8, (CC) hdc 3, (MC) hdc 9, (CC) hdc 2. [36 sts]

**Row 20:** (CC) ch 2, turn, hdc 1, (MC) hdc 11, (CC) hdc 3, (MC) hdc 6, (CC) hdc 3, (MC) hdc 11, (CC) hdc 1. [36 sts]

### Pro Tip

Worried about not counting the right amount of stitches for where to start your colorwork? Use stitch markers to mark where it begins. Then it's already counted and you don't have to count while you're crocheting!

**Row 21:** (MC) ch 2, turn, hdc 6, (CC) hdc 3, (MC) hdc 4, (CC) hdc 3, (MC) hdc 4, (CC) hdc 3, (MC) hdc 4, (CC) hdc 3, (MC) hdc 6. [36 sts]

**Row 22:** (MC) ch 2, turn, hdc 5, (CC) hdc 2, (MC) hdc 1, (CC) hdc 2, (MC) hdc 4, (CC) hdc 3, (MC) hdc 2, (CC) hdc 3, (MC) hdc 4, (CC) hdc 2, (MC) hdc 1, (CC) hdc 2, (MC) hdc 5. [36 sts]

**Row 23:** (MC) ch 2, turn, hdc 4, (CC) hdc 2, (MC) hdc 3, (CC) hdc 2, (MC) hdc 4, (CC) hdc 6, (MC) hdc 4, (CC) hdc 2, (MC) hdc 3, (CC) hdc 2, (MC) hdc 4. [36 sts]

**Row 24:** (MC) ch 2, turn, hdc 5, (CC) hdc 2, (MC) hdc 1, (CC) hdc 2, (MC) hdc 6, (CC) hdc 4, (MC) hdc 6, (CC) hdc 2, (MC) hdc 1, (CC) hdc 2, (MC) hdc 5. [36 sts]

**Row 25:** (MC) ch 2, turn, hdc 6, (CC) hdc 3, (MC) hdc 18, (CC) hdc 3, (MC) hdc 6. [36 sts]

**Row 26:** (MC) ch 2, turn, hdc 3, (CC) hdc 2, (MC) hdc 5, (CC) hdc 2, (MC) hdc 5, (CC) hdc 2, (MC) hdc 5, (CC) hdc 2, (MC) hdc 5, (CC) hdc 2, (MC) hdc 3. [36 sts]

**Row 27:** (MC) ch 2, turn, hdc 2, (CC) hdc 4, (MC) hdc 3, (CC) hdc 4, (MC) hdc 3, (CC) hdc 4, (MC) hdc 3, (CC) hdc 4, (MC) hdc 3, (CC) hdc 4, (MC) hdc 2. [36 sts]

**Row 28:** (MC) ch 2, turn, hdc 1, (CC) hdc 2, (MC) hdc 2, (CC) hdc 2, (MC) hdc 1, (CC) hdc 2, (MC) hdc 2, (CC) hdc 2, (MC) hdc 1, (CC) hdc 2, (MC) hdc 2, (CC) hdc 2, (MC) hdc 1, (CC) hdc 2, (MC) hdc 2, (CC) hdc 2, (MC) hdc 1, (CC) hdc 2, (MC) hdc 2, (CC) hdc 2, (MC) hdc 1. [36 sts]

**Row 29:** (CC) ch 2, turn, hdc 2, (MC) hdc 4, (CC) hdc 3, (MC) hdc 4, (CC) hdc 3, (MC) hdc 4, (CC) hdc 3, (MC) hdc 4, (CC) hdc 3, (MC) hdc 4, (CC) hdc 2. [36 sts]

**Row 30:** (MC) ch 2, turn, hdc 36. [36 sts]

Fasten off, and weave in the ends. On one of the panels, leave a long tail (approx. 20" [51 cm]) for sewing the two panels together.

### Assembly

Once you've finished both panels, it's time for assembly. Take your pillow form and lay the panels on it, one on each side of the form.

Pin the panels together around the form. Then, using the long tail you left for sewing on one of the panels, sew the panels together using your favorite seaming method (see pages 18-21).

*I love how geometric designs really stand out with crochet. With this hat design, you'll learn how to do tapestry crochet in the round. It will walk you through how to carry yarn in this mode, as well as how to offset the slanting that happens when working in the round.*

# Queen of Diamonds Hat

## Pattern Level: Beginner

**Gauge:** 4" x 4" (10 x 10 cm) square = 11 sc x 12 rows

**Gauge for Brim:** 4" x 4" (10 x 10 cm) square (worked in alternating rows of back loops only and front loops only) = 11 dc x 5 rows

**Hat Measurements:**
Circumference = 21" (53 cm)
Height = 8" (20 cm)

**Hook:** US L/11 8mm

**Yarn:** Lion Brand Color Made Easy (Yarn Weight 5 Bulky, 247 yds [226 m], 7 oz [200 g], 100 percent acrylic) in two colors:
• Pomegranate (MC)
• Millennial Pink (CC)

**Approximate Yarn Yardage:**
MC = 75 yds (68.5 m)
CC = 75 yds (68.5 m)

**Extra Materials:**
Yarn needle

**Abbreviations:**
ch = chain
dc = double crochet
sc = single crochet
blo = back loops only
flo = front loops only
st(s) = stitch(es)
sl st = slip stitch
rnd = round
MC = main color
CC = contrast color

## Chart

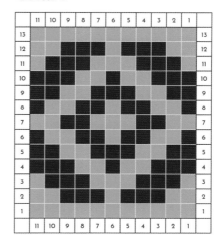

■ Main Color

▨ Contrast Color

For chart notes and how to read a chart, see pages 15–17.

# Queen of Diamonds Hat (Continued)

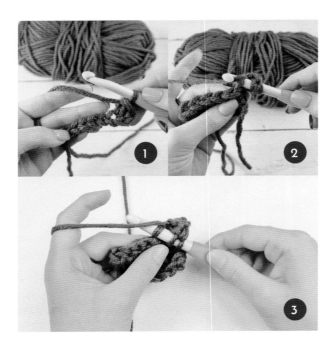

## Brim

Starting with MC, ch 8.

**Row 1:** starting in third ch from hook, dc 6. [6 sts]

**Row 2:** ch 2 (ch 2 at the beginning of each row does not count as a st), turn, dc across in the blo. [6 sts]

**Row 3:** ch 2, turn, dc across in the flo. [6 sts]

For the next 24 rows, repeat rows 2 and 3. You will have a total of 27 rows.

Once you're done with those rows, join the two ends of your brim right sides together with a sl st. Turn it right-side out, and then you'll move on to the body of the hat.

## Body of Hat

To switch to the CC, do your first ch st with the new color. Do not fasten off the MC. We will be using it after the first rnd. The first rnd sets up the base of the sc that we'll be using to make the rest of the hat.

**Rnd 1:** (CC) ch 1 (ch 1 at the beginning of the rnd does not count as a st), sc around the top of the brim of the hat (working approximately 2 sts in each row at the end of the brim) to make 55 sc around, then join with sl st to ch 1 at beginning of rnd. [55 sts]

You'll now work the rest of the hat through the blo. This helps offset the slanting that occurs when doing colorwork in the rnd. You can use the chart on page 32 to work alongside the written pattern below.

**Rnd 2:** (CC) ch 1, *sc 2, (MC) sc 3, (CC) sc 1, (MC) sc 3, (CC) sc 2, repeat from * 4 more times, join with sl st to ch 1 at beginning of rnd. [55 sts]

**Rnd 3:** (CC) ch 1, *sc 1, (MC) sc 3, (CC) sc 3, (MC) sc 3, (CC) sc 1, repeat from * 4 more times, join with sl st to ch 1 at beginning of rnd. [55 sts]

**Rnd 4:** (MC) ch 1, *sc 3, (CC) sc 2, (MC) sc 1, (CC) sc 2, (MC) sc 3, repeat from * 4 more times, join with sl st to ch 1 at beginning of rnd. [55 sts]

> **Pro Tip**
>
> Feel like your hat is bunching while you're crocheting? Check your tension! If you're pulling your yarn too tight while carrying it, the yarn can be too taught and cause the hat to bunch up. Loosen up your tension slightly and it will take the bunching away.

**Rnd 5:** (MC) ch 1, *sc 2, (CC) sc 2, (MC) sc 3, (CC) sc 2, (MC) sc 2, repeat from * 4 more times, join with sl st to ch 1 at beginning of rnd. [55 sts]

**Rnd 6:** (MC) ch 1, *sc 1, (CC) sc 2, (MC) sc 2, (CC) sc 1, (MC) sc 2, (CC) sc 2, (MC) sc 1, repeat from * 4 more times, join with sl st to ch 1 at beginning of rnd. [55 sts]

**Rnd 7:** (CC) ch 1, *sc 2, (MC) sc 2, (CC) sc 3, (MC) sc 2, (CC) sc 2, repeat from * 4 more times, join with sl st to ch 1 at beginning of rnd. [55 sts]

**Rnd 8:** (MC) ch 1, *sc 1, (CC) sc 2, (MC) sc 2, (CC) sc 1, (MC) sc 2, (CC) sc 2, (MC) sc 1, repeat from * 4 more times, join with sl st to ch 1 at beginning of rnd. [55 sts]

**Rnd 9:** (MC) ch 1, *sc 2, (CC) sc 2, (MC) sc 3, (CC) sc 2, (MC) sc 2, repeat from * 4 more times, join with sl st to ch 1 at beginning of rnd. [55 sts]

**Rnd 10:** (MC) ch 1, *sc 3, (CC) sc 2, (MC) sc 1, (CC) sc 2, (MC) sc 3, repeat from * 4 more times, join with sl st to ch 1 at beginning of rnd. [55 sts]

**Rnd 11:** (CC) ch 1, *sc 1, (MC) sc 3, (CC) sc 3, (MC) sc 3, (CC) sc 1, repeat from * 4 more times, join with sl st to ch 1 at beginning of rnd. [55 sts]

**Rnd 12:** (CC) ch 1, *sc 2, (MC) sc 3, (CC) sc 1, (MC) sc 3, (CC) sc 2, repeat from * 4 more times, join with sl st to ch 1 at beginning of rnd. [55 sts]

**Rnds 13 to 18:** (CC) ch 1, sc around, join with sl st to ch 1 at beginning of rnd. [55 sts]

Fasten off, leaving a long tail for sewing the hat closed.

To close up the hat, thread the long tail through a yarn needle and sew a basting stitch (see page 21) around the top of the hat, then pull closed. Fasten off once the hat is closed and weave in the ends.

## Attaching a Pom-Pom (Optional)

If you would like to add a faux fur pom-pom, as pictured in the sample, here is how you can do it. Position the pom-pom at the top of the hat, over the hole where you closed up the hat. Sew the pom-pom on top using an embroidery needle and thread, or if it has a snap closure position it on there and secure it. You can also make a pom-pom from yarn using a pom-pom maker and sew it in the same position.

*The Feathers in the Wind Shawl is one of my favorite designs in this book! I saw a beautiful colorwork knitted sweater done using a similar feather design and thought it would look amazing in crochet. This shawl is a great pattern to start using decreases mixed with colorwork and has a simple construction to make it great for colorwork beginners. With just a few simple techniques, you can make this amazing shawl!*

# Feathers in the Wind Shawl

## Pattern Level: Intermediate

**Gauge:** 4″ x 4″ (10 x 10 cm) square = 14 hdc x 9 rows

**Dimensions:** 63″ (160 cm) along the top and 24.5″ (62 cm) deep

**Hook:** US J/10 6mm

**Yarn:** Lion Brand Heartland (Yarn Weight 4 Medium, 251 yds [230 m], 5 oz [142 g], 100 percent acrylic) in two colors:
- Yosemite (MC)
- Great Sand Dunes (CC)

**Approximate Yarn Yardage:**
MC = 502 yds (459 m)
CC = 251 yds (230 m)

**Abbreviations:**
ch = chain
st(s) = stitch(es)
hdc = half double crochet
hdc dec = half double crochet two together
yo = yarn over
MC = main color
CC = contrast color

The chart on pages 42–45 can be used to make the pattern, or you can use the written pattern.

## Shawl

Starting with MC, ch 223.

**Row 1:** (MC) starting in third ch from the hook, hdc 221.

**Rows 2 and 3:** (MC) ch 2 (ch 2 at the beginning of the row throughout the pattern does not count as a st), turn, hdc dec 2, hdc to last 4 sts, hdc dec 2, on last hdc dec of row 3 switch to CC on the last yo. [213 sts]

**Rows 4 and 5:** (CC) ch 2, turn, hdc dec 2, hdc to last 4 sts, hdc dec 2, on last hdc dec of row 5 switch to MC on the last yo of the last hdc dec. [205 sts]

Starting in the next row, you will carry the unused color through the stitches until you need it.

**Row 6:** (MC) ch 2, turn, hdc dec 2, hdc 27, (CC) hdc 1, (MC) hdc 10, *(CC) hdc 1, (MC) hdc 11, repeat from * 9 more times, (CC) hdc 1, (MC) hdc 10, (CC) hdc 1, (MC) hdc to last 4 sts, hdc dec 2. [201 sts]

**Row 7:** (MC) ch 2, turn, hdc dec 2, hdc 25, (CC) hdc 1, (MC) hdc 10, *(CC) hdc 1, (MC) hdc 11, repeat from * 9 more times, (CC) hdc 1, (MC) hdc 10, (CC) hdc 1, (MC) hdc to last 4 sts, hdc dec 2. [197 sts]

**Row 8:** (MC) ch 2, turn, hdc dec 2, hdc 22, (CC) hdc 3, (MC) hdc 8, *(CC) hdc 3, (MC) hdc 9, repeat from * 9 more times, (CC) hdc 3, (MC) hdc 8, (CC) hdc 3, (MC) hdc to last 4 sts, hdc dec 2. [193 sts]

**Row 9:** (MC) ch 2, turn, hdc dec 2, hdc 19, (CC) hdc 5, (MC) hdc 6, *(CC) hdc 5, (MC) hdc 7, repeat from * 9 more times, (CC) hdc 5, (MC) hdc 6, (CC) hdc 5, (MC) hdc to last 4 sts, hdc dec 2. [189 sts]

**Pro Tip**

If you won't be needing the contrast color at the end of the row, you don't have to carry it all the way. Just leave it at the stitch where you will need it next, and then use it again in the next row.

**Row 10:** (MC) ch 2, turn, hdc dec 2, hdc 17, (CC) hdc 1, (MC) hdc 1, (CC) hdc 1, (MC) hdc 1, (CC) hdc 1, (MC) hdc 5, *(CC) hdc 2, (MC) hdc 1, (CC) hdc 1, (MC) hdc 1, (CC) hdc 2, (MC) hdc 5, repeat from * 10 more times, (CC) hdc 1, (MC) hdc 1, (CC) hdc 1, (MC) hdc 1, (CC) hdc 1, (MC) hdc to last 4 sts, hdc dec 2. [185 sts]

**Row 11:** (MC) ch 2, turn, hdc dec 2, hdc 16, (CC) hdc 3, (MC) hdc 8, *(CC) hdc 3, (MC) hdc 9, repeat from * 9 more times, (CC) hdc 3, (MC) hdc 8, (CC) hdc 3, (MC) hdc to last 4 sts, hdc dec 2. [181 sts]

**Row 12:** (MC) ch 2, turn, hdc dec 2, hdc 13, (CC) hdc 5, (MC) hdc 5, *(CC) hdc 7, (MC) hdc 5, repeat from * 10 more times, (CC) hdc 5, (MC) hdc to last 4 sts, hdc dec 2. [177 sts]

**Row 13:** (MC) ch 2, turn, hdc dec 2, hdc 11, (CC) hdc 1, (MC) hdc 1, (CC) hdc 1, (MC) hdc 1, (CC) hdc 1, *(MC) hdc 5, (CC) hdc 1, (MC) hdc 2, (CC) hdc 1, (MC) hdc 2, (CC) hdc 1, repeat from * 10 more times, (MC) hdc 5, (CC) hdc 1, (MC) hdc 1, (CC) hdc 1, (MC) hdc 1, (CC) hdc 1, (MC) hdc 11, hdc dec 2. [173 sts]

**Row 14:** (MC) ch 2, turn, hdc dec 2, hdc 10, (CC) hdc 3, *(MC) hdc 7, (CC) hdc 5, repeat from * 10 times, (MC) hdc 7, (CC) hdc 3, (MC) hdc to last 4 sts, hdc dec 2. [169 sts]

**Row 15:** (MC) ch 2, turn, hdc dec 2, hdc 7, (CC) hdc 1, (MC) hdc 1, (CC) hdc 1, (MC) hdc 1, (CC) hdc 1, *(MC) hdc 5, (CC) hdc 2, (MC) hdc 1, (CC) hdc 1, (MC) hdc 1, (CC) hdc 2, repeat from * 10 more times, (MC) hdc 5, (CC) hdc 1, (MC) hdc 1, (CC) hdc 1, (MC) hdc 1, (CC) hdc 1, (MC) hdc 7, hdc dec 2. [165 sts]

**Row 16:** (MC) ch 2, turn, hdc dec 2, hdc 6, (CC) hdc 3, (MC) hdc 6, *(CC) hdc 1, (MC) hdc 2, (CC) hdc 1, (MC) hdc 2, (CC) hdc 1, (MC) hdc 5, repeat from * 9 more times, (CC) hdc 1, (MC) hdc 2, (CC) hdc 1, (MC) hdc 2, (CC) hdc 1, (MC) hdc 6, (CC) hdc 3, (MC) hdc 6, hdc dec 2. [161 sts]

**Row 17:** (MC) ch 2, turn, hdc dec 2, hdc 5, (CC) hdc 1, (MC) hdc 8, (CC) hdc 5, *(MC) hdc 7, (CC) hdc 5, repeat from * 9 more times, (MC) hdc 8, (CC) hdc 1, (MC) hdc to last 4 sts, hdc dec 2. [157 sts]

**Row 18:** (MC) ch 2, turn, hdc dec 2, hdc 12, *(CC) hdc 1, (MC) hdc 1, (CC) hdc 1, (MC) hdc 1, (CC) hdc 1, (MC) hdc 7, repeat from * 9 more times, (CC) hdc 1, (MC) hdc 1, (CC) hdc 1, (MC) hdc 1, (CC) hdc 1, (MC) hdc to last 4 sts, hdc dec 2. [153 sts]

**Row 19:** (MC) ch 2, turn, hdc dec 2, hdc 11, *(CC) hdc 3, (MC) hdc 9, repeat from * 9 more times, (CC) hdc 3, (MC) hdc to last 4 sts, hdc dec 2. [149 sts]

**Row 20:** (MC) ch 2, turn, hdc dec 2, hdc 10, (CC) hdc 1, *(MC) hdc 11, (CC) hdc 1, repeat from * 9 more times, (MC) hdc to last 4 sts, hdc dec 2. [145 sts]

**Rows 21 and 22:** (MC) ch 2, turn, hdc dec 2, hdc to last 4 sts, hdc dec 2, on last hdc dec of row 22 switch to CC on the last yo of the last hdc dec. [137 sts]

**Rows 23 and 24:** (CC) ch 2, turn, hdc dec 2, hdc to last 4 sts, hdc dec 2. [129 sts]

**Row 25:** (CC) ch 2, turn, hdc dec 2, *(MC) hdc 1, (CC) hdc 2, (MC) hdc 2, (CC) hdc 2, repeat from * 16 more times, (MC) hdc 1, (CC) hdc 1, hdc dec 1, (MC) hdc dec 1. [125 sts]

**Row 26:** (CC) ch 2, turn, hdc dec 2, hdc 1, *(MC) hdc 4, (CC) hdc 3, repeat from * 15 times, (MC) hdc 4, (CC) hdc dec 2, switch to MC on last yo. [121 sts]

# Feathers in the Wind Shawl (Continued)

**Row 27:** (MC) ch 2, turn, hdc dec 2, hdc 3, *(CC) hdc 1, (MC) hdc 6, repeat from * 14 more times, (CC) hdc 1, (MC) hdc 4, hdc dec 2. [117 sts]

**Row 28:** (MC) ch 2, turn, hdc dec 2, hdc 1, *(CC) hdc 3, (MC) hdc 4, repeat from * 14 more times, (CC) hdc 3, (MC) hdc dec 2. [113 sts]

**Row 29:** (CC) ch 2, turn, hdc dec 1, (MC) hdc dec 1, *(CC) hdc 2, (MC) hdc 2, (CC) hdc 2, (MC) hdc 1, repeat from * 14 more times, (CC) hdc dec 2. [109 sts]

**Rows 30 and 31:** (CC) ch 2, turn, hdc dec 2, hdc to last 4 sts, hdc dec 2, on last hdc dec of row 31 switch to MC on the last yo of the last hdc dec. [101 sts]

**Rows 32 and 33:** (MC) ch 2, turn, hdc dec 2, hdc to last 4 sts, hdc dec 2, on last hdc dec of row 33 switch to CC on the last yo of the last hdc dec. [93 sts]

**Rows 34 and 35:** (CC) ch 2, turn, hdc dec 2, hdc to last 4 sts, hdc dec 2, on last hdc dec of row 35 switch to MC on the last yo of the last hdc dec. [85 sts]

**Row 36:** (MC) ch 2, turn, hdc dec 2, hdc 27, (CC) hdc 1, *(MC) hdc 10, (CC) hdc 1, repeat from * 1 more time, (MC) hdc to last 4 sts, hdc dec 2. [81 sts]

**Row 37:** (MC) ch 2, turn, hdc dec 2, hdc 25, *(CC) hdc 1, (MC) hdc 10, repeat from * 1 more time, (CC) hdc 1, (MC) hdc to last 4 sts, hdc dec 2. [77 sts]

**Row 38:** (MC) ch 2, turn, hdc dec 2, hdc 22, *(CC) hdc 3, (MC) hdc 8, repeat from * 1 more time, (CC) hdc 3, (MC) hdc to last 4 sts, hdc dec 2. [73 sts]

**Row 39:** (MC) ch 2, turn, hdc dec 2, hdc 19, *(CC) hdc 5, (MC) hdc 6, repeat from * 1 more time, (CC) hdc 5, (MC) hdc to last 4 sts, hdc dec 2. [69 sts]

**Row 40:** (MC) ch 2, turn, hdc dec 2, hdc 17, (CC) hdc 1, (MC) hdc 1, (CC) hdc 1, (MC) hdc 1, (CC) hdc 1, (MC) hdc 5, (CC) hdc 2, (MC) hdc 1, (CC) hdc 1, (MC) hdc 1, (CC) hdc 2, (MC) hdc 5, (CC) hdc 1, (MC) hdc 1, (CC) hdc 1, (MC) hdc 1, (CC) hdc 1, (MC) hdc to last 4 sts, hdc dec 2. [65 sts]

**Row 41:** (MC) ch 2, turn, hdc dec 2, hdc 16, *(CC) hdc 3, (MC) hdc 8, repeat from * 1 more time, (CC) hdc 3, (MC) hdc to last 4 sts, hdc dec 2. [61 sts]

**Row 42:** (MC) ch 2, turn, hdc dec 2, hdc 13, (CC) hdc 5, (MC) hdc 5, (CC) hdc 7, (MC) hdc 5, (CC) hdc 5, (MC) hdc to last 4 sts, hdc dec 2. [57 sts]

**Row 43:** (MC) ch 2, turn, hdc dec 2, hdc 11, (CC) hdc 1, (MC) hdc 1, (CC) hdc 1, (MC) hdc 1, (CC) hdc 1, (MC) hdc 5, (CC) hdc 1, (MC) hdc 2, (CC) hdc 1, (MC) hdc 2, (CC) hdc 1, (MC) hdc 5, (CC) hdc 1, (MC) hdc 1, (CC) hdc 1, (MC) hdc 1, (CC) hdc 1, (MC) hdc to last 4 sts, hdc dec 2. [53 sts]

**Row 44:** (MC) ch 2, turn, hdc dec 2, hdc 10, (CC) hdc 3, (MC) hdc 7, (CC) hdc 5, (MC) hdc 7, (CC) hdc 3, (MC) hdc to last 4 sts, hdc dec 2. [49 sts]

**Row 45:** (MC) ch 2, turn, hdc dec 2, hdc 7, (CC) hdc 1, (MC) hdc 1, (CC) hdc 1, (MC) hdc 1, (CC) hdc 1, (MC) hdc 5, (CC) hdc 2, (MC) hdc 1, (CC) hdc 1, (MC) hdc 1, (CC) hdc 2, (MC) hdc 5, (CC) hdc 1, (MC) hdc 1, (CC) hdc 1, (MC) hdc 1, (CC) hdc 1, (MC) hdc to last 4 sts, hdc dec 2. [45 sts]

**Row 46:** (MC) ch 2, turn, hdc dec 2, hdc 6, (CC) hdc 3, (MC) hdc 6, (CC) hdc 1, (MC) hdc 2, (CC) hdc 1, (MC) hdc 2, (CC) hdc 1, (MC) hdc 6, (CC) hdc 3, (MC) hdc to last 4 sts, hdc dec 2. [41 sts]

**Row 47:** (MC) ch 2, turn, hdc dec 2, hdc 5, (CC) hdc 1, (MC) hdc 8, (CC) hdc 5, (MC) hdc 8, (CC) hdc 1, (MC) hdc to last 4 sts, hdc dec 2. [37 sts]

**Row 48:** (MC) ch 2, turn, hdc dec 2, hdc 12, (CC) hdc 1, (MC) hdc 1, (CC) hdc 1, (MC) hdc 1, (CC) hdc 1, (MC) hdc to last 4 sts, hdc dec 2. [33 sts]

**Row 49:** (MC) ch 2, turn, hdc dec 2, hdc 11, (CC) hdc 3, (MC) hdc to last 4 sts, hdc dec 2. [29 sts]

**Row 50:** (MC) ch 2, turn, hdc dec 2, hdc 10, (CC) hdc 1, (MC) hdc to last 4 sts, hdc dec 2. [25 sts]

**Row 51:** (CC) ch 2, turn, hdc dec 2, hdc across to last 4 sts, hdc dec 2. [21 sts]

Fasten off the CC, and continue using the MC.

**Rows 52 through 55:** (MC) ch 2, turn, hdc dec 2, hdc to last 4 sts, hdc dec 2. [5 sts]

Fasten off, and weave in the ends.

## Tassels (optional)

To create tassels on the ends of your shawl, begin by taking your CC and cutting about 16 strands that are 8" (20 cm) long. Then take all of the strands and create a U shape with them. Pull the U through one of the corners of the shawl, then pull the strands of the yarn through the U. Pull it tight till the strands are secure, and you'll have one tassel. Repeat on the opposite corner as well.

## Charts

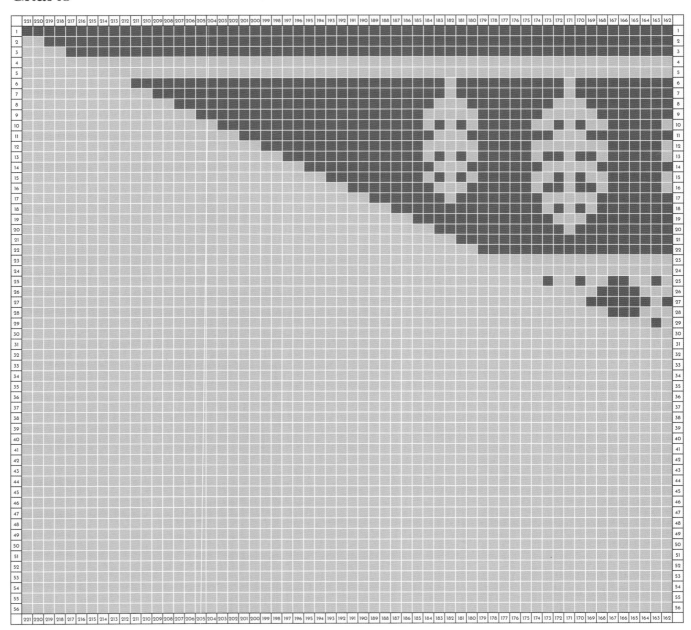

# Feathers in the Wind Shawl (Continued)

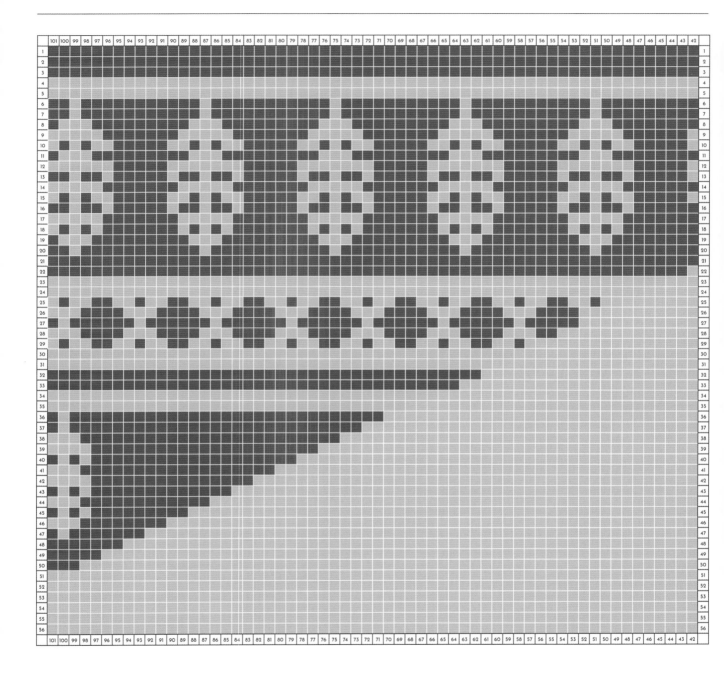

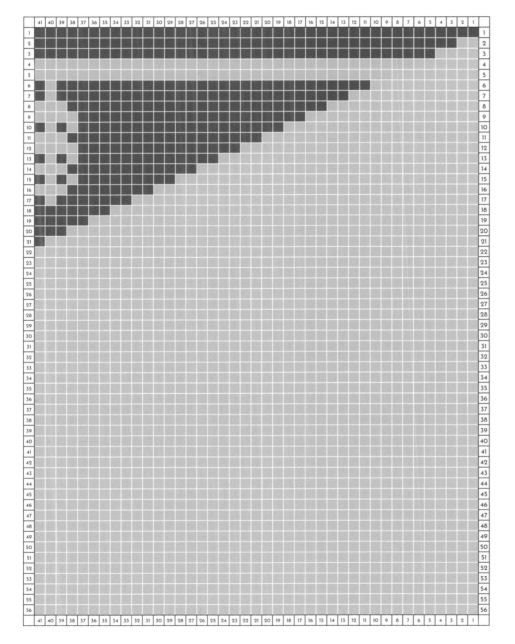

Main Color

Contrast Color

No Stitches

For chart notes and how to read a chart, see pages 15-17.

*The Desert Diamonds Top was inspired by terra-cotta tiles and pots that use simple diamonds to create something beautiful. If you've never made a crochet garment before, this is a great one to start with! This top has short sleeves, or can even be made with no sleeves at all. It is designed to be close fitting and flattering on your body. I used panel construction that is all worked in one piece so that you can work flat, with just the right amount of ease to make it drape. While experimenting with tapestry crochet, I found that working a garment flat really helps minimize any complicated techniques. You might just get hooked on garments after making this one!*

# Desert Diamonds Top

## Pattern Level: Beginner

**Gauge:** 4" x 4" (10 x 10 cm) square = 16 sc x 18 rows

**Sizes:** XS (S, M, L, XL, 2X, 3X, 4X, 5X)

**Finished Bust Measurements:**
- 32 (34, 38, 42, 46, 50, 54, 58, 62)"
- 81 (86, 96.5, 106.5, 116.5, 127, 137, 147, 157.5) cm

**Finished Length Measurements:**
- 22 (23, 23, 23.5, 24, 24, 24, 25, 25)"
- 55.5 (58.5, 58.5, 60, 61, 61, 61, 63.5, 63.5) cm

**Hook:** US J/10 6mm

**Yarn:**
- Lion Brand Jeans (Yarn Weight 4 Medium, 246 yds [225 m], 3.5 oz [100 g], 100 percent acrylic) in Top Stitch (MC)
- Lion Brand Jeans Colors (Yarn Weight 4 Medium, 246 yds [225 m], 3.5 oz [100 g], 100 percent acrylic) in Khaki (CC)

**Approximate Yarn Yardage:**

MC = 984 (1230, 1230, 1476, 1476, 1722, 1722, 1968, 2214) yds (900 [1125, 1125, 1350, 1350, 1575, 1575, 1800, 2024] m)

CC = 400 (400, 400, 450, 450, 450, 500, 500, 500) yds (366 [366, 366, 411, 411, 411, 457, 457, 457] m)

**Extra Materials:**

Yarn needle

**Abbreviations:**

ch = chain

st(s) = stitch(es)

sl st = slip stitch

sk = skip

sc = single crochet

MC = main color

CC = contrast color

# Desert Diamonds Top (Continued)

## Chart

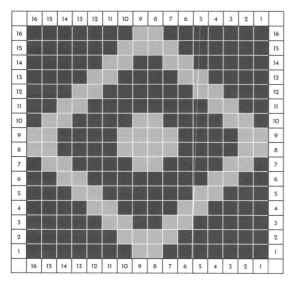

■ Main Color

▨ Contrast Color

For chart notes and how to read a chart, see pages 15-17.

## Front Panel

Starting with MC, ch 63 (69, 77, 81, 93, 101, 109, 117, 125).

**Row 1:** starting in second ch from the hook, sc 62 (68, 76, 80, 92, 100, 108, 116, 124).

**Rows 2 through 5:** ch 1 (ch 1 at the beginning of the row does not count as a st throughout the rest of the pattern), turn, sc across. [62 (68, 76, 80, 92, 100, 108, 116, 124) sts]

**Rows 6 and 7:** using CC, ch 1, turn, sc across. [62 (68, 76, 80, 92, 100, 108, 116, 124) sts]

You will now start using the chart on this page to do the colorwork portions of the pattern.

**Row 8:** (See above photo) starting with MC, ch 1, turn, sc 2 (5, 7, 2, 8, 2, 6, 5, 4), *crochet row 1 of the chart, sc 5 (5, 7, 4, 4, 4, 4, 2, 4), repeat from * 1 (1, 1, 2, 2, 3, 3, 4, 4) time(s), crochet row 1 of the chart, sc 2 (5, 7, 2, 8, 2, 6, 5, 4). [62 (68, 76, 80, 92, 100, 108, 116, 124) sts]

**Rows 9 through 23:** repeat row 8, and as you do each row move up one row of the chart. [62 (68, 76, 80, 92, 100, 108, 116, 124) sts]

**Rows 24 and 25:** using CC, ch 1, turn, sc across. [62 (68, 76, 80, 92, 100, 108, 116, 124) sts]

**Rows 26 through 35:** using MC, ch 1, turn, sc across. [62 (68, 76, 80, 92, 100, 108, 116, 124) sts]

In the following rounds, follow the instructions listed for your chosen size.

### Sizes XS through XL:

Repeat rows 6 through 35 once, then rows 6 through 25 once. When finished, fasten off the CC.

**Next 3 (8, 8, 10, 12) rows:** using MC, ch 1, turn, sc across. [62 (68, 76, 80, 92) sts]

Sizes XS through XL, move on to the neckline.

### Sizes 2XL through 5XL:

Repeat rows 6 through 35 two more times. When finished, fasten off the CC. Sizes 2XL through 3XL move on to the neckline. Sizes 4XL and 5XL continue the next steps.

### Sizes 4XL and 5XL:

**Next 5 rows:** using MC, ch 1, turn, sc across. [116 (124) sts]

Do not fasten off the MC. We'll now begin forming the neckline.

You still have the front number of rows the same for all sizes at 87 rows = 19.3" (49 cm). The back rows you have listed at either 87 rows = 19.3" (49 cm) or 116 rows = 25.78" (65.5 cm). To get the lengths mentioned here, at your row gauge you should have 99 (104, 104, 106, 108, 108, 108, 113, 113) rows.

## Neckline

**Row 1:** ch 1, turn, sc 20 (20, 20, 20, 25, 25, 30, 30, 30). To create the neckline you'll do the following ch sts and then sk stitches across to the other side of the piece. ch 22 (28, 36, 40, 42, 50, 48, 56, 64), (see above photo) sk 22 (28, 36, 40, 42, 50, 48, 56, 64) sts, starting in next st, sc 20 (20, 20, 20, 25, 25, 30, 30, 30) to end of row.

Do not fasten off the MC. We'll now begin working the back panel off of this row.

## Back Panel

**Row 1:** ch 1, turn, sc across including in each ch st from the neckline.

**Rows 2 through 99 (104, 104, 106, 108, 108, 108, 113, 113):** ch 1, turn, sc across. [62 (68, 76, 80, 92, 100, 108, 116, 124) sts]

Fasten off the yarn, weave in the ends and continue on with Seaming on the next page.

# Desert Diamonds Top (Continued)

## Seaming

Once the panels of your top are finished, it's time to seam them together. See pages 18–21 for different seaming methods you can use. I prefer to use the mattress stitch (page 19), which creates an invisible seam. You could also use a sc or sl st join, or a whip stitch. If you are using a seaming method like the mattress stitch, you will put wrong sides together to seam, but if it's a method like sl st or sc then you will do right sides together. Measure down from the top of the panels approximately 6 (6.5, 7, 7.5, 8, 8.5, 9, 9.5, 10)″ or 15 (16.5, 18, 19, 20, 21.5, 23, 24, 25.5) cm, and mark with a pin or stitch marker. Seam along each side from the bottom to the stitch marker. That will form the armholes for both sides. Once both sides are seamed, fasten off and weave in the ends.

## Sleeves (optional)

Work sleeves off of the armholes created from seaming on each side.

Using the MC, join yarn with a sl st to the seam at the bottom of the armhole (see photo above).

**Rnd 1:** ch 1, sc 48 (52, 56, 60, 64, 68, 72, 76, 80) around the armhole, join with sl st to ch 1 at beginning of rnd. [48 (52, 56, 60, 64, 68, 72, 76, 80) sts]

**Rnds 2 through 20:** ch 1, turn, sc around, join with sl st to ch 1 at beginning of rnd. [48 (52, 56, 60, 64, 68, 72, 76, 80) sts]

If you would like the sleeves to be longer, you can continue the last rnds until the sleeves reach the desired length.

Once the sleeves have reached your desired length, fasten off and weave in the ends. Repeat on the other armhole.

*The Trailing Vines Cardigan is inspired by the long and winding vines of the jungle. I love when trees have vines snaking down them, and I wanted to create a crochet cardigan that would feature them. This cardigan gives the fresh and rejuvenating feeling of plant life. It's perfect to pair with your favorite jeans and blouse, or even a cute summer dress. Its flowing drape and lightweight yarn makes it a great cardigan for warm weather. My favorite part about this cardigan is that it looks a lot more complicated than what it actually is. It uses the basic crochet and tapestry crochet techniques (page 24) to create a stylish cardigan with stunning colorwork.*

# Trailing Vines Cardigan

## Pattern Level: Intermediate

**Gauge:** 4" x 4" (10 x 10 cm) square = 18 sc x 19 rows

**Sizes:** XS (S, M, L, XL, 2X, 3X, 4X, 5X)

**Finished Bust Measurements:**
- 31 (34, 38, 42, 46, 50, 54, 58, 62)"
- 79 (86, 96.5, 106.5, 117, 127, 137, 147, 157.5) cm

**Finished Length Measurements:**
- 22 (23, 23, 23, 24, 24, 24, 25, 25)"
- 56 (58.5, 58.5, 58.5, 61, 61, 61, 63.5, 63.5) cm

**Finished Arm Length Measurements:**
- 16.5 (17, 17, 17.5, 17.5, 18, 18, 18.5, 18.5)"
- 42 (43, 43, 44.5, 44.5, 45.5, 45.5, 47, 47) cm

**Hook:** US 7 4.5mm

**Yarn:** Lion Brand Coboo (Yarn Weight 3 Light, 232 yds [212 m], 3.5 oz [100 g], 50 percent cotton, 50 percent rayon from bamboo) in two colors:
- Beige (MC)
- Olive (CC)

**Approximate Yarn Yardage:**

MC = 700 (871, 1028, 1185, 1300, 1400, 1727, 1780, 1950) yds (640 [796, 940, 1084, 1189, 1280, 1579, 1628, 1783] m)

CC = 464 (464, 464, 550, 550, 550, 696, 696, 696) yds (424 [424, 424, 503, 503, 503, 637, 637, 637] m)

**Extra Materials:**

Yarn needle

**Abbreviations:**

ch = chain

st(s) = stitch(es)

sl st = slip stitch

dc = double crochet

sc = single crochet

dec = decrease (single crochet 2 together)

rnd = round

MC = main color

CC = contrast color

yo = yarn over

# Trailing Vines Cardigan (Continued)

## Chart

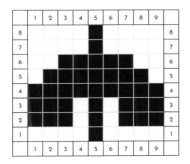

☐ Contrast Color

■ Main Color

For chart notes and how to read a chart, see pages 15–17.

## Back Panel

Starting with the CC, ch 73 (82, 91, 100, 109, 118, 127, 136, 145).

**Row 1:** starting in second ch from hook, sc in each sc across. [72 (81, 90, 99, 108, 117, 126, 135, 144) sts]

**Rows 2 through 5:** ch 1 (ch 1 at the beginning of the row does not count as a st throughout the rest of the pattern), turn, sc across, on last yo of the last sc, switch to MC. [72 (81, 90, 99, 108, 117, 126, 135, 144) sts]

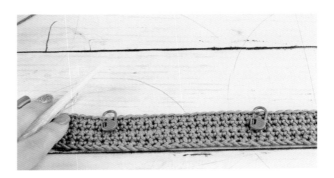

### Pro Tip

When starting the first row of colorwork, I recommend adding stitch markers where you'll start each part of colorwork, especially on garments that have more frequent color changes. This helps you to keep track of all of the color changes and gives you a solid foundation for the chart without having to count stitches while you're crocheting.

You will now begin using the chart on this page for the colorwork portions of the pattern.

**Row 6:** ch 1, turn, sc 9 (11, 9, 9, 10, 12, 11, 12, 14), *crochet row 1 of chart that starts the vine, sc 6 (8, 7, 9, 7, 8, 7, 8, 9), repeat from * 2 (2, 3, 3, 4, 5, 5, 5) times, crochet row 1 of chart that starts the vine, sc 9 (10, 8, 9, 9, 11, 10, 12, 13). [72 (81, 90, 99, 108, 117, 126, 135, 144) sts]

**Row 7:** ch 1, turn, sc 9 (10, 8, 9, 10, 11, 10, 12, 13), * crochet row 2 of chart that starts the vine, sc 6 (8, 7, 9, 7, 8, 7, 8, 9), repeat from * 2 (2, 2, 3, 3, 4, 4, 5, 5, 5) times, crochet row 1 of chart that starts the vine, sc 9 (11, 9, 9, 11, 12, 11, 12, 14). [72 (81, 90, 99, 108, 117, 126, 135, 144) sts]

**Rows 8 through 14:** repeat rows 6 to 7, and as you do each row move up one row of the chart.

Repeat rows 6 through 14 until the back panel reaches 22 (23, 23, 23, 24, 24, 24, 25, 25)", 56 (58.5, 58.5, 58.5, 61, 61, 61, 63.5, 63.5) cm or desired length. Fasten off and weave in the ends.

## Front Panel 1

Starting with CC, ch 37 (46, 46, 55, 55, 64, 64, 73, 81).

**Row 1:** starting in second st from hook, sc 36 (45, 45, 54, 54, 63, 63, 72, 80).

**Rows 2 through 5:** ch 1, turn, sc across.

### Sizes XS and S

**Row 6:** ch 1, turn, (MC) sc 18 (27), crochet row 1 of chart that starts the vine, (MC) sc 3 (3), (CC) sc 6. [36 (45) sts]

**Row 7:** ch 1, turn, (CC) sc 6, (MC) sc 3, crochet row 2 of chart that starts the vine, (MC) sc 18 (27). [36 (45) sts]

Repeat rows 6 and 7, moving up in the chart until panel reaches 22 (23)", 56 (58.5) cm or desired length. Make sure that the front and back panels are the same length.

### Sizes M through 2XL

**Row 6:** (MC) ch 1, turn, sc 19 (27, 26, 28), crochet row 1 of chart that starts the vine, (MC) sc 9 (9, 9, 16), (CC) sc 8 (9, 10, 10). [45 (54, 54, 63) sts]

**Row 7:** ch 1, turn, (CC) sc 8 (9, 10, 10), (MC) sc 9 (9, 9, 16), crochet row 2 of chart that starts the vine, sc 19 (27, 26, 28). [45 (54, 54, 63) sts]

Repeat rows 6 and 7, moving up in the chart until panel reaches 23 (23, 24, 24)", 58.5 (58.5, 61, 61) cm or desired length. Make sure that the front and back panels are the same length.

### Sizes 3XL through 5XL

**Row 6:** (MC) ch 1, turn, sc 42 (46, 49), crochet row 1 of chart that starts the vine, (MC) sc 7 (8, 9), (CC) sc 5 (9, 13). [63 (72, 80) sts]

**Row 7:** ch 1, turn, (CC) sc 5 (9, 13), (MC) sc 7 (8, 9), crochet row 2 of chart that starts the vine, sc 42 (46, 49). [63 (72, 80) sts]

Repeat rows 6 and 7, moving up in the chart until panel reaches 24 (25, 25)", 61 (63.5, 63.5) cm or desired length. Make sure that the front and back panels are the same length.

## Front Panel 2

Starting with CC, ch 37 (46, 46, 55, 55, 64, 64, 73, 81).

**Row 1:** starting in second st from hook, sc 36 (45, 45, 54, 54, 63, 63, 72, 80).

**Rows 2 through 5:** ch 1, turn, sc across.

### Sizes XS and S

**Row 6:** ch 1, turn, (CC) sc 6, (MC) sc 3, crochet row 1 of chart that starts the vine, (MC) sc 18 (27). [36 (45) sts]

**Row 7:** ch 1, turn, (MC) sc 18 (27), crochet row 2 of chart that starts the vine, (MC) sc 3 (3), (CC) sc 6. [36 (45) sts]

Repeat rows 6 and 7, moving up in the chart until panel reaches 22 (23)", 56 (58.5) cm or desired length. Make sure that the front and back panels are the same length.

### Sizes M through 2XL

**Row 6:** ch 1, turn, (CC) sc 8 (9, 10, 10), (MC) sc 9 (9, 9, 16), crochet row 2 of chart that starts the vine, sc 19 (27, 26, 28). [45 (54, 54, 63) sts]

**Row 7:** ch 1, turn, sc 19 (27, 26, 28), crochet row 1 of chart that starts the vine, (MC) sc 9 (9, 9, 16), (CC) sc 8 (9, 10, 10). [45 (54, 54, 63) sts]

Repeat rows 6 and 7, moving up in the chart until panel reaches 23 (23, 24, 24)", 58.5 (58.5, 61, 61) cm or desired length. Make sure that the front and back panels are the same length.

### Sizes 3XL through 5XL

**Row 6:** ch 1, turn, (CC) sc 5 (9, 13), (MC) sc 7 (8, 9), crochet row 2 of chart that starts the vine, sc 42 (46, 49). [63 (72, 80) sts]

**Row 7:** ch 1, turn, sc 42 (46, 49), crochet row 1 of chart that starts the vine, (MC) sc 7 (8, 9), (CC) sc 5 (9, 13). [63 (72, 80) sts]

Repeat rows 6 and 7, moving up in the chart until panel reaches 24 (25, 25)", 61 (63.5, 63.5) cm or desired length. Make sure that the front and back panels are the same length.

Fasten off and weave in ends.

## Seaming Panels

Once you have finished the back and both front panels, it's time to seam them together. See pages 18-21 for different seaming methods to use. Depending on what type of seaming method you've chosen, you'll put either right sides together or wrong sides together. For my sweater, I used a sl st seam (page 21), so I put the right sides together.

Before you seam, you'll position the front panels on top of the back panels. With each front panel, you will want the edge that has CC sts as trim to be the center of the front. See photo on page 57 for reference.

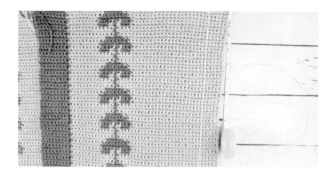

(See left photo) On the left and right sides, measure down approximately 6 (7, 7, 8, 8, 9, 9, 10, 10)" or 15 (18, 18, 20, 20, 23, 23, 25.5, 25.5) cm from the top. Mark that point, and you will work up to this point when seaming the sides. This helps form the armhole.

From the outside edges, seam the top edges together until you get to 2 stitches past the vine on each front panel.

## Sleeves

(See right photo) Join MC with a sl st to the seam that stops at the underarm.

**Rnd 1:** ch 1, dc 54 (63, 63, 72, 72, 81, 81, 90, 90) around the armhole, join with sl st to ch 1 at beginning of rnd. [54 (63, 63, 72, 72, 81, 81, 90, 90) sts]

**Rnds 2 through 4:** ch 1, dc around, join with sl st to ch 1 at beginning of rnd. [54 (63, 63, 72, 72, 81, 81, 90, 90) sts]

**Rnd 5:** ch 1, *dc 4 (5, 5, 6, 6, 7, 7, 8, 8), dec 1, repeat from * around, join with sl st to ch 1 at beginning of rnd. [45 (54, 54, 63, 63, 72, 72, 81, 81) sts]

**Rnds 6 through 10:** ch 1, dc around, join with sl st to ch 1 at beginning of rnd. [45 (54, 54, 63, 63, 72, 72, 81, 81) sts]

**Rnd 11:** ch 1, *dc 3 (4, 4, 5, 5, 6, 6, 7, 7), dec 1, repeat from * around, join with sl st to ch 1 at beginning of rnd. [36 (45, 45, 54, 54, 63, 63, 72, 72) sts]

**Rnds 12 through 16:** ch 1, dc around, join with sl st to ch 1 at beginning of rnd. [36 (45, 45, 54, 54, 63, 63, 72, 72) sts]

**Rnd 17:** ch 1, *dc 2 (3, 3, 4, 4, 5, 5, 6, 6), dec 1, repeat from * around, join with sl st to ch 1 at beginning of rnd. [27 (36, 36, 45, 45, 54, 54, 63, 63) sts]

**Rnd 18:** ch 1, dc around, join with sl st to ch 1 at beginning of rnd. [27 (36, 36, 45, 45, 54, 54, 63, 63) sts]

Repeat the last rnd until the sleeve reaches the desired length.

Fasten off. Weave in the ends. Repeat for other sleeve.

*The Flower Paisley Blanket was inspired by floral blankets that I had as a girl, but with a boho and modern twist. Often I'll see blankets similar to this one at expensive stores selling them for $400, which I definitely can't afford. Why not just crochet one? This blanket continues using the tapestry crochet techniques we've used in the previous patterns in this chapter, but on a larger scale. This pattern might look like it's more complicated, but it is perfect practice to solidify your tapestry crochet skills. The large scale provides a lot of space to help you master carrying yarn and changing back and forth between two colors. Plus, it's one of the coziest blankets you'll make!*

# Flower Paisley Blanket

## Pattern Level: Intermediate

**Gauge:** 4" x 4" (10 x 10 cm) square = 10 dc x 6 rows

**Dimensions:** 57" (145 cm) wide x 60" (152.5 cm) long

**Hook:** US L/11 8mm

**Yarn:** Lion Brand Color Made Easy (Yarn Weight 5 Bulky, 247 yds [226 m], 7 oz [200 g], 100 percent acrylic) in two colors:
- Mineral Yellow (MC)
- Alabaster (CC)

**Approximate Yarn Yardage:**

MC = 1482 yds (1355 m)

CC = 494 yds (452 m)

**Abbreviations:**

ch = chain

st(s) = stitch(es)

dc = double crochet

MC = main color

CC = contrast color

To crochet this blanket, you can use just the chart (pages 71-73), by chaining the amount of sts needed, and then crocheting each stitch while using the chart for reference. The written version of the pattern is written out below for your convenience, if you would prefer that instead. I personally like using just the chart to crochet blankets.

# Flower Paisley Blanket (Continued)

With the MC, ch 145.

**Row 1:** (MC) starting in third ch from hook, dc 143. [143 sts]

**Rows 2 through 4:** (MC) ch 2 (ch 2 at the beginning of the row does not count as a st throughout the rest of the pattern), turn, dc across. [143 sts]

**Row 5:** (MC) ch 2, turn, dc 8, (CC) dc 3, (MC) dc 3, (CC) dc 3, (MC) dc 9, [(CC) dc 1, (MC) dc 5] 15 times, (CC) dc 1, (MC) dc 9, (CC) dc 3, (MC) dc 3, (CC) dc 3, (MC) dc 8. [143 sts]

**Row 6:** (MC) ch 2, turn, dc 7, (CC) dc 1, (MC) dc 3, (CC) dc 1, (MC) dc 1, (CC) dc 1, (MC) dc 2, (CC) dc 2, (MC) dc 7, [(CC) dc 3, (MC) dc 3] 15 times, (CC) dc 3, (MC) dc 7, (CC) dc 1, (MC) dc 3, (CC) dc 1, (MC) dc 1, (CC) dc 1, (MC) dc 2, (CC) dc 2, (MC) dc 7. [143 sts]

**Row 7:** (MC) ch 2, turn, dc 6, (CC) dc 1, (MC) dc 5, (CC) dc 1, (MC) dc 5, (CC) dc 1, (MC) dc 7, [(CC) dc 1, (MC) dc 5] 15 times, (CC) dc 1, (MC) dc 7, (CC) dc 1, (MC) dc 5, (CC) dc 1, (MC) dc 5, (CC) dc 1, (MC) dc 6. [143 sts]

**Row 8:** (MC) ch 2, turn, dc 5, (CC) dc 1, (MC) dc 6, (CC) dc 1, (MC) dc 6, (CC) dc 1, (MC) dc 3, [(CC) dc 1, (MC) dc 5] 16 times, (CC) dc 1, (MC) dc 3, (CC) dc 1, (MC) dc 6, (CC) dc 1, (MC) dc 6, (CC) dc 1, (MC) dc 5. [143 sts]

**Row 9:** (MC) ch 2, turn, dc 5, (CC) dc 1, (MC) dc 6, (CC) dc 1, (MC) dc 6, (CC) dc 1, (MC) dc 3, [(CC) dc 1, (MC) dc 5] 16 times, (CC) dc 1, (MC) dc 3, (CC) dc 1, (MC) dc 6, (CC) dc 1, (MC) dc 6, (CC) dc 1, (MC) dc 5. [143 sts]

**Row 10:** (MC) ch 2, turn, dc 4, (CC) dc 1, (MC) dc 1, (CC) dc 2, (MC) dc 3, (CC) dc 3, (MC) dc 3, (CC) dc 2, (MC) dc 1, (CC) dc 1, (MC) dc 18, (CC) dc 10, (MC) dc 45, (CC) dc 10, (MC) dc 18, (CC) dc 1, (MC) dc 1, (CC) dc 2, (MC) dc 3, (CC) dc 3, (MC) dc 3, (CC) dc 2, (MC) dc 1, (CC) dc 1, (MC) dc 4. [143 sts]

**Row 11:** (MC) ch 2, turn, dc 3, (CC) dc 1, (MC) dc 4, (CC) dc 1, (MC) dc 1, (CC) dc 2, (MC) dc 1, (CC) dc 2, (MC) dc 1, (CC) dc 1, (MC) dc 4, (CC) dc 1, (MC) dc 16, (CC) dc 2, (MC) dc 9, (CC) dc 1, (MC) dc 14, (CC) dc 5, (MC) dc 5, (CC) dc 5, (MC) dc 14, (CC) dc 1, (MC) dc 9, (CC) dc 2, (MC) dc 16, (CC) dc 1, (MC) dc 4, (CC) dc 1, (MC) dc 1, (CC) dc 2, (MC) dc 1, (CC) dc 2, (MC) dc 1, (CC) dc 1, (MC) dc 4, (CC) dc 1, (MC) dc 3. [143 sts]

**Row 12:** (MC) ch 2, turn, dc 3, (CC) dc 1, (MC) dc 5, (CC) dc 2, (MC) dc 3, (CC) dc 2, (MC) dc 5, (CC) dc 1, (MC) dc 15, (CC) dc 1, (MC) dc 2, (CC) dc 8, (MC) dc 2, (CC) dc 1, (MC) dc 12, (CC) dc 1, (MC) dc 5, (CC) dc 1, (MC) dc 3, (CC) dc 1, (MC) dc 5, (CC) dc 1, (MC) dc 12, (CC) dc 1, (MC) dc 2, (CC) dc 8, (MC) dc 2, (CC) dc 1, (MC) dc 15, (CC) dc 1, (MC) dc 5, (CC) dc 2, (MC) dc 3, (CC) dc 2, (MC) dc 5, (CC) dc 1, (MC) dc 3. [143 sts]

**Row 13:** (MC) ch 2, turn, dc 4, (CC) dc 1, (MC) dc 5, (CC) dc 1, (MC) dc 3, (CC) dc 1, (MC) dc 5, (CC) dc 1, (MC) dc 15, (CC) dc 1, (MC) dc 2, (CC) dc 1, (MC) dc 8, (CC) dc 1, (MC) dc 2, (CC) dc 1, (MC) dc 10, (CC) dc 1, (MC) dc 3, (CC) dc 1, (MC) dc 3, (CC) dc 1, (MC) dc 1, (CC) dc 1, (MC) dc 2, (CC) dc 1, (MC) dc 1, (CC) dc 1, (MC) dc 2, (CC) dc 1, (MC) dc 10, (CC) dc 1, (MC) dc 2, (CC) dc 1, (MC) dc 8, (CC) dc 1, (MC) dc 2, (CC) dc 1, (MC) dc 15, (CC) dc 1, (MC) dc 5, (CC) dc 1, (MC) dc 3, (CC) dc 1, (MC) dc 5, (CC) dc 1, (MC) dc 4. [143 sts]

**Row 14:** (MC) ch 2, turn, dc 3, (CC) dc 1, (MC) dc 5, (CC) dc 2, (MC) dc 3, (CC) dc 2, (MC) dc 5, (CC) dc 1, (MC) dc 13, (CC) dc 1, (MC) dc 2, (CC) dc 1, (MC) dc 5, (CC) dc 1, (MC) dc 4, (CC) dc 1, (MC) dc 1, (CC) dc 2, (MC) dc 8, (CC) dc 1, (MC) dc 2, (CC) dc 1, (MC) dc 4, (CC) dc 2, (MC) dc 1, (CC) dc 2, (MC) dc 4, (CC) dc 1, (MC) dc 2, (CC) dc 1, (MC) dc 8, (CC) dc 2, (MC) dc 1, (CC) dc 1, (MC) dc 4, (CC) dc 1, (MC) dc 5, (CC) dc 1, (MC) dc 2, (CC) dc 1, (MC) dc 13, (CC) dc 1, (MC) dc 5, (CC) dc 2, (MC) dc 3, (CC) dc 2, (MC) dc 5, (CC) dc 1, (MC) dc 3. [143 sts]

**Row 15:** (MC) ch 2, turn, dc 3, (CC) dc 1, (MC) dc 4, (CC) dc 1, (MC) dc 1, (CC) dc 2, (MC) dc 1, (CC) dc 2, (MC) dc 1, (CC) dc 1, (MC) dc 4, (CC) dc 1, (MC) dc 12, (CC) dc 1, (MC) dc 2, (CC) dc 1, (MC) dc 5, (CC) dc 1, (MC) dc 2, (CC) dc 1, (MC) dc 3, (CC) dc 1, (MC) dc 1, (CC) dc 1, (MC) dc 8, [(CC) dc 1, (MC) dc 1] 3 times, (CC) dc 1, (MC) dc 2, (CC) dc 1, (MC) dc 1, (CC) dc 1, (MC) dc 2, (CC) dc 1, (MC) dc 1, (CC) dc 1, (MC) dc 3, (CC) dc 1, (MC) dc 8, (CC) dc 1, (MC) dc 1, (CC) dc 1, (MC) dc 3, (CC) dc 1, (MC) dc 2, (CC) dc 1, (MC) dc 5, (CC) dc 1, (MC) dc 2, (CC) dc 1, (MC) dc 12, (CC) dc 1, (MC) dc 4, (CC) dc 1, (MC) dc 1, (CC) dc 2, (MC) dc 1, (CC) dc 2, (MC) dc 1, (CC) dc 1, (MC) dc 4, (CC) dc 1, (MC) dc 3. [143 sts]

**Row 16:** (MC) ch 2, turn, dc 4, (CC) dc 1, (MC) dc 1, (CC) dc 2, (MC) dc 3, (CC) dc 3, (MC) dc 3, (CC) dc 2, (MC) dc 1, (CC) dc 1, (MC) dc 12, (CC) dc 1, (MC) dc 2, (CC) dc 1, (MC) dc 3, (CC) dc 1, (MC) dc 9, (CC) dc 1, (MC) dc 1, (CC) dc 1, (MC) dc 8, (CC) dc 1, (MC) dc 1, (CC) dc 1, (MC) dc 5, (CC) dc 1, (MC) dc 3, (CC) dc 1, (MC) dc 7, (CC) dc 1, (MC) dc 8, (CC) dc 1, (MC) dc 1, (CC) dc 1, (MC) dc 9, (CC) dc 1, (MC) dc 3, (CC) dc 1, (MC) dc 2, (CC) dc 1, (MC) dc 12, (CC) dc 1, (MC) dc 1, (CC) dc 2, (MC) dc 3, (CC) dc 3, (MC) dc 3, (CC) dc 2, (MC) dc 1, (CC) dc 1, (MC) dc 4. [143 sts]

**Row 17:** (MC) ch 2, turn, dc 5, (CC) dc 1, (MC) dc 6, (CC) dc 1, (MC) dc 6, (CC) dc 1, (MC) dc 13, (CC) dc 1, (MC) dc 1, (CC) dc 1, (MC) dc 2, [(CC) dc 1, (MC) dc 5] twice, (CC) dc 1, (MC) dc 1, (CC) dc 1, (MC) dc 8, (CC) dc 1, (MC) dc 2, (CC) dc 1, (MC) dc 1, (CC) dc 1, (MC) dc 1, (CC) dc 1, (MC) dc 5, (CC) dc 1, (MC) dc 2, (CC) dc 1, (MC) dc 3, (CC) dc 1, (MC) dc 8, (CC) dc 1, (MC) dc 1, (CC) dc 1, (MC) dc 5, (CC) dc 1, (MC) dc 5, (CC) dc 1, (MC) dc 2, (CC) dc 1, (MC) dc 1, (CC) dc 1, (MC) dc 13, (CC) dc 1, (MC) dc 6, (CC) dc 1, (MC) dc 6, (CC) dc 1, (MC) dc 5. [143 sts]

**Row 18:** (MC) ch 2, turn, dc 5, (CC) dc 1, (MC) dc 6, (CC) dc 1, (MC) dc 6, (CC) dc 1, (MC) dc 13, (CC) dc 1, (MC) dc 1, (CC) dc 1, (MC) dc 1, (CC) dc 1, (MC) dc 4, (CC) dc 1, (MC) dc 4, (CC) dc 1, (MC) dc 2, (CC) dc 1, (MC) dc 1, (CC) dc 1, (MC) dc 9, (CC) dc 1, (MC) dc 3, (CC) dc 2, (MC) dc 7, (CC) dc 1, (MC) dc 3, (CC) dc 2, (MC) dc 9, (CC) dc 1, (MC) dc 1, (CC) dc 1, (MC) dc 2, (CC) dc 1, (MC) dc 4, (CC) dc 1, (MC) dc 4, (CC) dc 1, (MC) dc 1, (CC) dc 1, (MC) dc 1, (CC) dc 1, (MC) dc 13, (CC) dc 1, (MC) dc 6, (CC) dc 1, (MC) dc 6, (CC) dc 1, (MC) dc 5. [143 sts]

# Flower Paisley Blanket (Continued)

**Row 19:** (MC) ch 2, turn, dc 6, (CC) dc 1, (MC) dc 5, (CC) dc 1, (MC) dc 5, (CC) dc 1, (MC) dc 14, (CC) dc 1, (MC) dc 1, (CC) dc 1, (MC) dc 2, (CC) dc 1, (MC) dc 10, (CC) dc 1, (MC) dc 1, (CC) dc 2, (MC) dc 9, (CC) dc 1, (MC) dc 1, (CC) dc 2, (MC) dc 1, (CC) dc 1, (MC) dc 7, (CC) dc 1, (MC) dc 2, (CC) dc 1, (MC) dc 1, (CC) dc 1, (MC) dc 9, (CC) dc 2, (MC) dc 1, (CC) dc 1, (MC) dc 10, (CC) dc 1, (MC) dc 2, (CC) dc 1, (MC) dc 1, (CC) dc 1, (MC) dc 14, (CC) dc 1, (MC) dc 5, (CC) dc 1, (MC) dc 5, (CC) dc 1, (MC) dc 6. [143 sts]

**Row 20:** (MC) ch 2, turn, dc 7, (CC) dc 1, (MC) dc 3, (CC) dc 1, (MC) dc 1, (CC) dc 1, (MC) dc 3, (CC) dc 1, (MC) dc 15, (CC) dc 1, (MC) dc 1, (CC) dc 1, (MC) dc 4, (CC) dc 1, (MC) dc 3, (CC) dc 1, (MC) dc 2, (CC) dc 1, (MC) dc 1, (CC) dc 1, (MC) dc 1, (CC) dc 1, (MC) dc 11, (CC) dc 1, (MC) dc 2, (CC) dc 1, (MC) dc 9, (CC) dc 1, (MC) dc 2, (CC) dc 1, (MC) dc 11, (CC) dc 1, (MC) dc 1, (CC) dc 1, (MC) dc 1, (CC) dc 1, (MC) dc 2, (CC) dc 1, (MC) dc 3, (CC) dc 1, (MC) dc 4, (CC) dc 1, (MC) dc 1, (CC) dc 1, (MC) dc 15, (CC) dc 1, (MC) dc 3, (CC) dc 1, (MC) dc 1, (CC) dc 1, (MC) dc 3, (CC) dc 1, (MC) dc 7. [143 sts]

**Row 21:** (MC) ch 2, turn, dc 8, (CC) dc 3, (MC) dc 3, (CC) dc 3, (MC) dc 16, (CC) dc 1, (MC) dc 1, (CC) dc 1, (MC) dc 2, (CC) dc 1, (MC) dc 9, (CC) dc 1, (MC) dc 2, (CC) dc 1, (MC) dc 11, (CC) dc 1, (MC) dc 2, (CC) dc 1, (MC) dc 9, (CC) dc 1, (MC) dc 2, (CC) dc 1, (MC) dc 11, (CC) dc 1, (MC) dc 2, (CC) dc 1, (MC) dc 9, (CC) dc 1, (MC) dc 2, (CC) dc 1, (MC) dc 1, (CC) dc 1, (MC) dc 16, (CC) dc 3, (MC) dc 3, (CC) dc 3, (MC) dc 8. [143 sts]

**Pro Tip**

When there are rows in which you don't need the contrast color at the end of the row, you don't have to carry it all the way. Instead, you can drop the yarn after the last stitch you need it, and then pick it up to use again in the next row (see photo above).

**Row 22:** (MC) ch 2, turn, dc 33, (CC) dc 1, (MC) dc 1, (CC) dc 1, (MC) dc 7, (CC) dc 1, (MC) dc 3, (CC) dc 1, (MC) dc 2, (CC) dc 1, (MC) dc 13, (CC) dc 1, (MC) dc 1, (CC) dc 1, (MC) dc 9, (CC) dc 1, (MC) dc 1, (CC) dc 1, (MC) dc 13, (CC) dc 1, (MC) dc 2, (CC) dc 1, (MC) dc 3, (CC) dc 1, (MC) dc 7, (CC) dc 1, (MC) dc 1, (CC) dc 1, (MC) dc 33. [143 sts]

**Row 23:** (MC) ch 2, turn, dc 33, (CC) dc 1, (MC) dc 1, (CC) dc 1, (MC) dc 2, (CC) dc 1, (MC) dc 2, (CC) dc 1, (MC) dc 1, (CC) dc 1, (MC) dc 2, (CC) dc 1, (MC) dc 2, (CC) dc 1, (MC) dc 14, (CC) dc 1, (MC) dc 2, (CC) dc 1, (MC) dc 7, (CC) dc 1, (MC) dc 2, (CC) dc 1, (MC) dc 14, (CC) dc 1, (MC) dc 2, (CC) dc 1, (MC) dc 2, (CC) dc 1, (MC) dc 1, (CC) dc 1, (MC) dc 2, (CC) dc 1, (MC) dc 2, (CC) dc 1, (MC) dc 1, (CC) dc 1, (MC) dc 33. [143 sts]

**Row 24:** (MC) ch 2, turn, dc 34, (CC) dc 1, (MC) dc 1, (CC) dc 1, (MC) dc 2, (CC) dc 1, (MC) dc 5, (CC) dc 1, (MC) dc 2, (CC) dc 1, (MC) dc 16, (CC) dc 1, (MC) dc 2, (CC) dc 1, (MC) dc 5, (CC) dc 1, (MC) dc 2, (CC) dc 1, (MC) dc 16, (CC) dc 1, (MC) dc 2, (CC) dc 1, (MC) dc 5, (CC) dc 1, (MC) dc 2, (CC) dc 1, (MC) dc 1, (CC) dc 1, (MC) dc 34. [143 sts]

**Row 25:** (MC) ch 2, turn, dc 34, (CC) dc 1, (MC) dc 2, (CC) dc 1, (MC) dc 6, (CC) dc 1, (MC) dc 2, (CC) dc 1, (MC) dc 18, (CC) dc 2, (MC) dc 7, (CC) dc 2, (MC) dc 18, (CC) dc 1, (MC) dc 2, (CC) dc 1, (MC) dc 6, (CC) dc 1, (MC) dc 2, (CC) dc 1, (MC) dc 34. [143 sts]

**Row 26:** (MC) ch 2, turn, dc 35, (CC) dc 1, (MC) dc 1, (CC) dc 1, (MC) dc 2, (CC) dc 1, (MC) dc 2, (CC) dc 1, (MC) dc 2, (CC) dc 1, (MC) dc 49, (CC) dc 1, (MC) dc 2, (CC) dc 1, (MC) dc 2, (CC) dc 1, (MC) dc 2, (CC) dc 1, (MC) dc 1, (CC) dc 1, (MC) dc 35. [143 sts]

**Row 27:** (MC) ch 2, turn, dc 35, (CC) dc 1, (MC) dc 1, (CC) dc 1, (MC) dc 5, (CC) dc 1, (MC) dc 1, (CC) dc 1, (MC) dc 51, (CC) dc 1, (MC) dc 1, (CC) dc 1, (MC) dc 5, (CC) dc 1, (MC) dc 1, (CC) dc 1, (MC) dc 35. [143 sts]

**Row 28:** (MC) ch 2, turn, dc 36, (CC) dc 1, (MC) dc 1, (CC) dc 1, (MC) dc 3, (CC) dc 1, (MC) dc 2, (CC) dc 1, (MC) dc 19, (CC) dc 5, (MC) dc 3, (CC) dc 5, (MC) dc 19, (CC) dc 1, (MC) dc 2, (CC) dc 1, (MC) dc 3, (CC) dc 1, (MC) dc 1, (CC) dc 1, (MC) dc 36. [143 sts]

**Row 29:** (MC) ch 2, turn, dc 36, (CC) dc 1, (MC) dc 1, (CC) dc 1, (MC) dc 1, (CC) dc 1, (MC) dc 1, (CC) dc 1, (MC) dc 1, (CC) dc 1, (MC) dc 19, (CC) dc 3, (MC) dc 3, (CC) dc 1, (MC) dc 1, (CC) dc 1, (MC) dc 4, (CC) dc 2, (MC) dc 19, (CC) dc 1, (MC) dc 1, (CC) dc 1, (MC) dc 1, (CC) dc 1, (MC) dc 1, (CC) dc 1, (MC) dc 1, (CC) dc 1, (MC) dc 36. [143 sts]

**Row 30:** (MC) ch 2, turn, dc 37, (CC) dc 2, (MC) dc 3, (CC) dc 3, (MC) dc 19, (CC) dc 1, (MC) dc 6, (CC) dc 1, (MC) dc 6, (CC) dc 1, (MC) dc 19, (CC) dc 3, (MC) dc 3, (CC) dc 2, (MC) dc 37. [143 sts]

**Row 31:** (MC) ch 2, turn, dc 37, (CC) dc 2, (MC) dc 4, (CC) dc 2, (MC) dc 19, (CC) dc 1, (MC) dc 6, (CC) dc 1, (MC) dc 6, (CC) dc 1, (MC) dc 19, (CC) dc 2, (MC) dc 4, (CC) dc 2, (MC) dc 37. [143 sts]

**Row 32:** (MC) ch 2, turn, dc 38, (CC) dc 2, (MC) dc 1, (CC) dc 1, (MC) dc 1, (CC) dc 2, (MC) dc 19, (CC) dc 1, (MC) dc 6, (CC) dc 1, (MC) dc 6, (CC) dc 1, (MC) dc 19, (CC) dc 2, (MC) dc 1, (CC) dc 1, (MC) dc 1, (CC) dc 2, (MC) dc 38. [143 sts]

# Flower Paisley Blanket (Continued)

**Row 33:** (MC) ch 2, turn, dc 38, (CC) dc 2, (MC) dc 4, (CC) dc 2, (MC) dc 13, (CC) dc 5, (MC) dc 7, (CC) dc 1, (MC) dc 7, (CC) dc 5, (MC) dc 13, (CC) dc 2, (MC) dc 4, (CC) dc 2, (MC) dc 38. [143 sts]

**Row 34:** (MC) ch 2, turn, dc 39, (CC) dc 2, (MC) dc 1, (CC) dc 1, (MC) dc 2, (CC) dc 1, (MC) dc 12, (CC) dc 2, (MC) dc 11, (CC) dc 1, (MC) dc 11, (CC) dc 2, (MC) dc 12, (CC) dc 1, (MC) dc 2, (CC) dc 1, (MC) dc 1, (CC) dc 2, (MC) dc 39. [143 sts]

**Row 35:** (MC) ch 2, turn, dc 22, (CC) dc 4, (MC) dc 13, (CC) dc 4, (MC) dc 1, (CC) dc 3, (MC) dc 10, (CC) dc 2, (MC) dc 12, (CC) dc 1, (MC) dc 12, (CC) dc 2, (MC) dc 10, (CC) dc 3, (MC) dc 1, (CC) dc 4, (MC) dc 12, (CC) dc 4, (MC) dc 23. [143 sts]

**Row 36:** (MC) ch 2, turn, dc 22, (CC) dc 1, (MC) dc 2, (CC) dc 1, (MC) dc 1, (CC) dc 2, (MC) dc 11, (CC) dc 2, (MC) dc 3, (CC) dc 2, (MC) dc 9, (CC) dc 2, (MC) dc 13, (CC) dc 1, (MC) dc 13, (CC) dc 2, (MC) dc 9, (CC) dc 2, (MC) dc 3, (CC) dc 2, (MC) dc 12, (CC) dc 2, (MC) dc 1, (CC) dc 1, (MC) dc 2, (CC) dc 1, (MC) dc 21. [143 sts]

**Row 37:** (MC) ch 2, turn, dc 20, (CC) dc 1, (MC) dc 7, (CC) dc 2, (MC) dc 10, (CC) dc 3, (MC) dc 1, (CC) dc 1, (MC) dc 1, (CC) dc 1, (MC) dc 9, (CC) dc 1, (MC) dc 9, (CC) dc 1, (MC) dc 1, (CC) dc 1, (MC) dc 2, (CC) dc 1, (MC) dc 2, (CC) dc 1, (MC) dc 1, (CC) dc 1, (MC) dc 9, (CC) dc 1, (MC) dc 9, (CC) dc 1, (MC) dc 1, (CC) dc 1, (MC) dc 1, (CC) dc 3, (MC) dc 9, (CC) dc 2, (MC) dc 7, (CC) dc 1, (MC) dc 21. [143 sts]

**Row 38:** (MC) ch 2, turn, dc 20, (CC) dc 1, (MC) dc 2, (CC) dc 1, (MC) dc 1, (CC) dc 1, (MC) dc 1, (CC) dc 1, (MC) dc 3, (CC) dc 2, (MC) dc 8, (CC) dc 3, (MC) dc 2, (CC) dc 2, (MC) dc 8, (CC) dc 3, (MC) dc 5, (CC) dc 1, (MC) dc 2, [(CC) dc 1, (MC) dc 1] 4 times, (CC) dc 1, (MC) dc 2, (CC) dc 1, (MC) dc 5, (CC) dc 3, (MC) dc 8, (CC) dc 2, (MC) dc 2, (CC) dc 3, (MC) dc 9, (CC) dc 2, (MC) dc 3, (CC) dc 1, (MC) dc 1, (CC) dc 1, (MC) dc 1, (CC) dc 1, (MC) dc 2, (CC) dc 1, (MC) dc 19. [143 sts]

**Row 39:** (MC) ch 2, turn, dc 19, [(CC) dc 1, (MC) dc 1] 3 times, (CC) dc 1, (MC) dc 3, (CC) dc 1, (MC) dc 2, (CC) dc 1, (MC) dc 9, (CC) dc 6, (MC) dc 7, (CC) dc 1, (MC) dc 2, (CC) dc 3, (MC) dc 2, (CC) dc 1, (MC) dc 1, (CC) dc 1, (MC) dc 2, (CC) dc 7, (MC) dc 2, (CC) dc 1, (MC) dc 1, (CC) dc 1, (MC) dc 2, (CC) dc 3, (MC) dc 2, (CC) dc 1, (MC) dc 7, (CC) dc 6, (MC) dc 8, (CC) dc 1, (MC) dc 2, (CC) dc 1, (MC) dc 3, [(CC) dc 1, (MC) dc 1] 3 times, (CC) dc 1, (MC) dc 20. [143 sts]

**Row 40:** (MC) ch 2, turn, dc 20, (CC) dc 1, (MC) dc 8, (CC) dc 3, (MC) dc 2, (CC) dc 1, (MC) dc 19, (CC) dc 1, (MC) dc 5, (CC) dc 2, (MC) dc 2, (CC) dc 1, (MC) dc 1, (CC) dc 4, (MC) dc 3, (CC) dc 4, (MC) dc 1, (CC) dc 1, (MC) dc 2, (CC) dc 2, (MC) dc 5, (CC) dc 1, (MC) dc 20, (CC) dc 1, (MC) dc 2, (CC) dc 3, (MC) dc 8, (CC) dc 1, (MC) dc 19. [143 sts]

**Row 41:** (MC) ch 2, turn, dc 19, (CC) dc 2, (MC) dc 1, (CC) dc 2, (MC) dc 2, (CC) dc 2, (MC) dc 3, (CC) dc 1, (MC) dc 1, (CC) dc 1, (MC) dc 20, (CC) dc 1, (MC) dc 7, (CC) dc 1, (MC) dc 2, (CC) dc 2, (MC) dc 9, (CC) dc 2, (MC) dc 2, (CC) dc 1, (MC) dc 7, (CC) dc 1, (MC) dc 19, (CC) dc 1, (MC) dc 1, (CC) dc 1, (MC) dc 3, (CC) dc 2, (MC) dc 2, (CC) dc 2, (MC) dc 1, (CC) dc 2, (MC) dc 20. [143 sts]

**Row 42:** (MC) ch 2, turn, dc 20, (CC) dc 1, (MC) dc 5, (CC) dc 1, (MC) dc 6, (CC) dc 1, (MC) dc 20, (CC) dc 1, (MC) dc 8, (CC) dc 3, (MC) dc 11, (CC) dc 3, (MC) dc 8, (CC) dc 1, (MC) dc 21, (CC) dc 1, (MC) dc 6, (CC) dc 1, (MC) dc 5, (CC) dc 1, (MC) dc 19. [143 sts]

**Row 43:** (MC) ch 2, turn, dc 20, (CC) dc 5, (MC) dc 29, (CC) dc 2, (MC) dc 9, (CC) dc 1, (MC) dc 11, (CC) dc 1, (MC) dc 9, (CC) dc 2, (MC) dc 28, (CC) dc 5, (MC) dc 21. [143 sts]

**Pro Tip**

You've got this! You're halfway through the pattern! Now the rest of the pattern is just mirroring what you've already done. If you're feeling fatigued, take a break and come back to crocheting this later. Sometimes a break is all you need to feel refreshed with a project.

**Row 44:** (MC) ch 2, turn, dc 55, (CC) dc 1, (MC) dc 7, (CC) dc 3, (MC) dc 11, (CC) dc 3, (MC) dc 7, (CC) dc 1, (MC) dc 55. [143 sts]

**Row 45:** (MC) ch 2, turn, dc 55, (CC) dc 1, (MC) dc 9, (CC) dc 1, (MC) dc 11, (CC) dc 1, (MC) dc 9, (CC) dc 1, (MC) dc 55. [143 sts]

**Row 46:** (MC) ch 2, turn, dc 55, (CC) dc 1, (MC) dc 9, (CC) dc 1, (MC) dc 11, (CC) dc 1, (MC) dc 9, (CC) dc 1, (MC) dc 55. [143 sts]

**Row 47:** (MC) ch 2, turn, dc 55, (CC) dc 1, (MC) dc 7, (CC) dc 3, (MC) dc 11, (CC) dc 3, (MC) dc 7, (CC) dc 1, (MC) dc 55. [143 sts]

**Row 48:** (MC) ch 2, turn, dc 21, (CC) dc 5, (MC) dc 28, (CC) dc 2, (MC) dc 9, (CC) dc 1, (MC) dc 11, (CC) dc 1, (MC) dc 9, (CC) dc 2, (MC) dc 29, (CC) dc 5, (MC) dc 20. [143 sts]

**Row 49:** (MC) ch 2, turn, dc 19, (CC) dc 1, (MC) dc 5, (CC) dc 1, (MC) dc 6, (CC) dc 1, (MC) dc 21, (CC) dc 1, (MC) dc 8, (CC) dc 3, (MC) dc 11, (CC) dc 3, (MC) dc 8, (CC) dc 1, (MC) dc 20, (CC) dc 1, (MC) dc 6, (CC) dc 1, (MC) dc 5, (CC) dc 1, (MC) dc 20. [143 sts]

**Row 50:** (MC) ch 2, turn, dc 20, (CC) dc 2, (MC) dc 1, (CC) dc 2, (MC) dc 2, (CC) dc 2, (MC) dc 3, (CC) dc 1, (MC) dc 1, (CC) dc 1, (MC) dc 19, (CC) dc 1, (MC) dc 7, (CC) dc 1, (MC) dc 2, (CC) dc 2, (MC) dc 9, (CC) dc 2, (MC) dc 2, (CC) dc 1, (MC) dc 7, (CC) dc 1, (MC) dc 20, (CC) dc 1, (MC) dc 1, (CC) dc 1, (MC) dc 3, (CC) dc 2, (MC) dc 2, (CC) dc 2, (MC) dc 1, (CC) dc 2, (MC) dc 19. [143 sts]

**Row 51:** (MC) ch 2, turn, dc 19, (CC) dc 1, (MC) dc 8, (CC) dc 3, (MC) dc 2, (CC) dc 1, (MC) dc 20, (CC) dc 1, (MC) dc 5, (CC) dc 2, (MC) dc 2, (CC) dc 1, (MC) dc 1, (CC) dc 4, (MC) dc 3, (CC) dc 4, (MC) dc 1, (CC) dc 1, (MC) dc 2, (CC) dc 2, (MC) dc 5, (CC) dc 1, (MC) dc 19, (CC) dc 1, (MC) dc 2, (CC) dc 3, (MC) dc 8, (CC) dc 1, (MC) dc 20. [143 sts]

# Flower Paisley Blanket (Continued)

**Row 52:** (MC) ch 2, turn, dc 20, (CC) dc 1, (MC) dc 1, (CC) dc 1, (MC) dc 1, (CC) dc 1, (MC) dc 1, (CC) dc 1, (MC) dc 3, (CC) dc 1, (MC) dc 2, (CC) dc 1, (MC) dc 8, (CC) dc 6, (MC) dc 7, (CC) dc 1, (MC) dc 2, (CC) dc 3, (MC) dc 2, (CC) dc 1, (MC) dc 1, (CC) dc 1, (MC) dc 2, (CC) dc 7, (MC) dc 2, (CC) dc 1, (MC) dc 1, (CC) dc 1, (MC) dc 2, (CC) dc 3, (MC) dc 2, (CC) dc 1, (MC) dc 7, (CC) dc 6, (MC) dc 9, (CC) dc 1, (MC) dc 2, (CC) dc 1, (MC) dc 3, (CC) dc 1, (MC) dc 1, (CC) dc 1, (MC) dc 1, (CC) dc 1, (MC) dc 1, (CC) dc 1, (MC) dc 19. [143 sts]

**Row 53:** (MC) ch 2, turn, dc 19, (CC) dc 1, (MC) dc 2, (CC) dc 1, (MC) dc 1, (CC) dc 1, (MC) dc 1, (CC) dc 1, (MC) dc 3, (CC) dc 2, (MC) dc 9, (CC) dc 3, (MC) dc 2, (CC) dc 2, (MC) dc 8, (CC) dc 3, (MC) dc 5, (CC) dc 1, (MC) dc 2, (CC) dc 1, (MC) dc 1, (CC) dc 1, (MC) dc 1, (CC) dc 1, (MC) dc 1, (CC) dc 1, (MC) dc 1, (CC) dc 1, (MC) dc 2, (CC) dc 1, (MC) dc 5, (CC) dc 3, (MC) dc 8, (CC) dc 2, (MC) dc 2, (CC) dc 3, (MC) dc 8, (CC) dc 2, (MC) dc 3, (CC) dc 1, (MC) dc 1, (CC) dc 1, (MC) dc 1, (CC) dc 1, (MC) dc 2, (CC) dc 1, (MC) dc 20. [143 sts]

**Row 54:** (MC) ch 2, turn, dc 21, (CC) dc 1, (MC) dc 7, (CC) dc 2, (MC) dc 9, (CC) dc 3, (MC) dc 1, (CC) dc 1, (MC) dc 1, (CC) dc 1, (MC) dc 9, (CC) dc 1, (MC) dc 9, (CC) dc 1, (MC) dc 1, (CC) dc 1, (MC) dc 2, (CC) dc 1, (MC) dc 2, (CC) dc 1, (MC) dc 1, (CC) dc 1, (MC) dc 9, (CC) dc 1, (MC) dc 9, (CC) dc 1, (MC) dc 1, (CC) dc 1, (MC) dc 1, (CC) dc 3, (MC) dc 10, (CC) dc 2, (MC) dc 7, (CC) dc 1, (MC) dc 20. [143 sts]

**Row 55:** (MC) ch 2, turn, dc 21, (CC) dc 1, (MC) dc 2, (CC) dc 1, (MC) dc 1, (CC) dc 2, (MC) dc 12, (CC) dc 2, (MC) dc 3, (CC) dc 2, (MC) dc 9, (CC) dc 2, (MC) dc 13, (CC) dc 1, (MC) dc 13, (CC) dc 2, (MC) dc 9, (CC) dc 2, (MC) dc 3, (CC) dc 2, (MC) dc 11, (CC) dc 2, (MC) dc 1, (CC) dc 1, (MC) dc 2, (CC) dc 1, (MC) dc 22. [143 sts]

**Row 56:** (MC) ch 2, turn, dc 23, (CC) dc 4, (MC) dc 12, (CC) dc 4, (MC) dc 1, (CC) dc 3, (MC) dc 10, (CC) dc 2, (MC) dc 12, (CC) dc 1, (MC) dc 12, (CC) dc 2, (MC) dc 10, (CC) dc 3, (MC) dc 1, (CC) dc 4, (MC) dc 13, (CC) dc 4, (MC) dc 22. [143 sts]

**Row 57:** (MC) ch 2, turn, dc 39, (CC) dc 2, (MC) dc 1, (CC) dc 1, (MC) dc 2, (CC) dc 1, (MC) dc 12, (CC) dc 2, (MC) dc 11, (CC) dc 1, (MC) dc 11, (CC) dc 2, (MC) dc 12, (CC) dc 1, (MC) dc 2, (CC) dc 1, (MC) dc 1, (CC) dc 2, (MC) dc 39. [143 sts]

**Row 58:** (MC) ch 2, turn, dc 38, (CC) dc 2, (MC) dc 4, (CC) dc 2, (MC) dc 13, (CC) dc 5, (MC) dc 7, (CC) dc 1, (MC) dc 7, (CC) dc 5, (MC) dc 13, (CC) dc 2, (MC) dc 4, (CC) dc 2, (MC) dc 38. [143 sts]

**Row 59:** (MC) ch 2, turn, dc 38, (CC) dc 2, (MC) dc 1, (CC) dc 1, (MC) dc 1, (CC) dc 2, (MC) dc 19, (CC) dc 1, (MC) dc 6, (CC) dc 1, (MC) dc 6, (CC) dc 1, (MC) dc 19, (CC) dc 2, (MC) dc 1, (CC) dc 1, (MC) dc 1, (CC) dc 2, (MC) dc 38. [143 sts]

**Row 60:** (MC) ch 2, turn, dc 37, (CC) dc 2, (MC) dc 4, (CC) dc 2, (MC) dc 19, (CC) dc 1, (MC) dc 6, (CC) dc 1, (MC) dc 6, (CC) dc 1, (MC) dc 19, (CC) dc 2, (MC) dc 4, (CC) dc 2, (MC) dc 37. [143 sts]

**Row 61:** (MC) ch 2, turn, dc 37, (CC) dc 2, (MC) dc 3, (CC) dc 3, (MC) dc 19, (CC) dc 1, (MC) dc 6, (CC) dc 1, (MC) dc 6, (CC) dc 1, (MC) dc 19, (CC) dc 3, (MC) dc 3, (CC) dc 2, (MC) dc 37. [143 sts]

**Row 62:** (MC) ch 2, turn, dc 36, (CC) dc 1, (MC) dc 1, (CC) dc 1, (MC) dc 1, (CC) dc 1, (MC) dc 1, (CC) dc 1, (MC) dc 1, (CC) dc 1, (MC) dc 19, (CC) dc 2, (MC) dc 4, (CC) dc 1, (MC) dc 1, (CC) dc 1, (MC) dc 3, (CC) dc 3, (MC) dc 19, (CC) dc 1, (MC) dc 1, (CC) dc 1, (MC) dc 1, (CC) dc 1, (MC) dc 1, (CC) dc 1, (MC) dc 1, (CC) dc 1, (MC) dc 36. [143 sts]

**Row 63:** (MC) ch 2, turn, dc 36, (CC) dc 1, (MC) dc 1, (CC) dc 1, (MC) dc 3, (CC) dc 1, (MC) dc 2, (CC) dc 1, (MC) dc 19, (CC) dc 5, (MC) dc 3, (CC) dc 5, (MC) dc 19, (CC) dc 1, (MC) dc 2, (CC) dc 1, (MC) dc 3, (CC) dc 1, (MC) dc 1, (CC) dc 1, (MC) dc 36. [143 sts]

**Row 64:** (MC) ch 2, turn, dc 35, (CC) dc 1, (MC) dc 1, (CC) dc 1, (MC) dc 5, (CC) dc 1, (MC) dc 1, (CC) dc 1, (MC) dc 51, (CC) dc 1, (MC) dc 1, (CC) dc 1, (MC) dc 5, (CC) dc 1, (MC) dc 1, (CC) dc 1, (MC) dc 35. [143 sts]

**Row 65:** (MC) ch 2, turn, dc 35, (CC) dc 1, (MC) dc 1, (CC) dc 1, (MC) dc 2, (CC) dc 1, (MC) dc 2, (CC) dc 1, (MC) dc 2, (CC) dc 1, (MC) dc 49, (CC) dc 1, (MC) dc 2, (CC) dc 1, (MC) dc 2, (CC) dc 1, (MC) dc 2, (CC) dc 1, (MC) dc 1, (CC) dc 1, (MC) dc 35. [143 sts]

**Row 66:** (MC) ch 2, turn, dc 34, (CC) dc 1, (MC) dc 2, (CC) dc 1, (MC) dc 6, (CC) dc 1, (MC) dc 2, (CC) dc 1, (MC) dc 18, (CC) dc 2, (MC) dc 7, (CC) dc 2, (MC) dc 18, (CC) dc 1, (MC) dc 2, (CC) dc 1, (MC) dc 6, (CC) dc 1, (MC) dc 2, (CC) dc 1, (MC) dc 34. [143 sts]

**Row 67:** (MC) ch 2, turn, dc 34, (CC) dc 1, (MC) dc 1, (CC) dc 1, (MC) dc 2, (CC) dc 1, (MC) dc 5, (CC) dc 1, (MC) dc 2, (CC) dc 1, (MC) dc 16, (CC) dc 1, (MC) dc 2, (CC) dc 1, (MC) dc 5, (CC) dc 1, (MC) dc 2, (CC) dc 1, (MC) dc 16, (CC) dc 1, (MC) dc 2, (CC) dc 1, (MC) dc 5, (CC) dc 1, (MC) dc 2, (CC) dc 1, (MC) dc 1, (CC) dc 1, (MC) dc 34. [143 sts]

**Row 68:** (MC) ch 2, turn, dc 33, (CC) dc 1, (MC) dc 1, (CC) dc 1, (MC) dc 2, (CC) dc 1, (MC) dc 2, (CC) dc 1, (MC) dc 1, (CC) dc 1, (MC) dc 2, (CC) dc 1, (MC) dc 2, (CC) dc 1, (MC) dc 14, (CC) dc 1, (MC) dc 2, (CC) dc 1, (MC) dc 7, (CC) dc 1, (MC) dc 2, (CC) dc 1, (MC) dc 14, (CC) dc 1, (MC) dc 2, (CC) dc 1, (MC) dc 2, (CC) dc 1, (MC) dc 1, (CC) dc 1, (MC) dc 2, (CC) dc 1, (MC) dc 2, (CC) dc 1, (MC) dc 1, (CC) dc 1, (MC) dc 33. [143 sts]

**Row 69:** (MC) ch 2, turn, dc 33, (CC) dc 1, (MC) dc 1, (CC) dc 1, (MC) dc 7, (CC) dc 1, (MC) dc 3, (CC) dc 1, (MC) dc 2, (CC) dc 1, (MC) dc 13, (CC) dc 1, (MC) dc 1, (CC) dc 1, (MC) dc 9, (CC) dc 1, (MC) dc 1, (CC) dc 1, (MC) dc 13, (CC) dc 1, (MC) dc 2, (CC) dc 1, (MC) dc 3, (CC) dc 1, (MC) dc 7, (CC) dc 1, (MC) dc 1, (CC) dc 1, (MC) dc 33. [143 sts]

**Row 70:** (MC) ch 2, turn, dc 8, (CC) dc 3, (MC) dc 3, (CC) dc 3, (MC) dc 16, (CC) dc 1, (MC) dc 1, (CC) dc 1, (MC) dc 2, (CC) dc 1, (MC) dc 9, (CC) dc 1, (MC) dc 2, (CC) dc 1, (MC) dc 11, (CC) dc 1, (MC) dc 2, (CC) dc 1, (MC) dc 9, (CC) dc 1, (MC) dc 2, (CC) dc 1, (MC) dc 11, (CC) dc 1, (MC) dc 2, (CC) dc 1, (MC) dc 9, (CC) dc 1, (MC) dc 2, (CC) dc 1, (MC) dc 1, (CC) dc 1, (MC) dc 16, (CC) dc 3, (MC) dc 3, (CC) dc 3, (MC) dc 8. [143 sts]

**Row 71:** (MC) ch 2, turn, dc 7, (CC) dc 1, (MC) dc 3, (CC) dc 1, (MC) dc 1, (CC) dc 1, (MC) dc 3, (CC) dc 1, (MC) dc 15, (CC) dc 1, (MC) dc 1, (CC) dc 1, (MC) dc 4, (CC) dc 1, (MC) dc 3, (CC) dc 1, (MC) dc 2, (CC) dc 1, (MC) dc 1, (CC) dc 1, (MC) dc 1, (CC) dc 1, (MC) dc 11, (CC) dc 1, (MC) dc 2, (CC) dc 1, (MC) dc 9, (CC) dc 1, (MC) dc 2, (CC) dc 1, (MC) dc 11, (CC) dc 1, (MC) dc 1, (CC) dc 1, (MC) dc 1, (CC) dc 1, (MC) dc 2, (CC) dc 1, (MC) dc 3, (CC) dc 1, (MC) dc 4, (CC) dc 1, (MC) dc 1, (CC) dc 1, (MC) dc 15, (CC) dc 1, (MC) dc 3, (CC) dc 1, (MC) dc 1, (CC) dc 1, (MC) dc 3, (CC) dc 1, (MC) dc 7. [143 sts]

# Flower Paisley Blanket (Continued)

**Row 72:** (MC) ch 2, turn, dc 6, (CC) dc 1, (MC) dc 5, (CC) dc 1, (MC) dc 5, (CC) dc 1, (MC) dc 14, (CC) dc 1, (MC) dc 1, (CC) dc 1, (MC) dc 2, (CC) dc 1, (MC) dc 10, (CC) dc 1, (MC) dc 1, (CC) dc 2, (MC) dc 9, (CC) dc 1, (MC) dc 1, (CC) dc 1, (MC) dc 2, (CC) dc 1, (MC) dc 7, (CC) dc 1, (MC) dc 1, (CC) dc 2, (MC) dc 1, (CC) dc 1, (MC) dc 9, (CC) dc 2, (MC) dc 1, (CC) dc 1, (MC) dc 10, (CC) dc 1, (MC) dc 2, (CC) dc 1, (MC) dc 1, (CC) dc 1, (MC) dc 14, (CC) dc 1, (MC) dc 5, (CC) dc 1, (MC) dc 5, (CC) dc 1, (MC) dc 6. [143 sts]

**Row 73:** (MC) ch 2, turn, dc 5, (CC) dc 1, (MC) dc 6, (CC) dc 1, (MC) dc 6, (CC) dc 1, (MC) dc 13, (CC) dc 1, (MC) dc 1, (CC) dc 1, (MC) dc 1, (CC) dc 1, (MC) dc 4, (CC) dc 1, (MC) dc 4, (CC) dc 1, (MC) dc 2, (CC) dc 1, (MC) dc 1, (CC) dc 1, (MC) dc 9, (CC) dc 2, (MC) dc 3, (CC) dc 1, (MC) dc 7, (CC) dc 2, (MC) dc 3, (CC) dc 1, (MC) dc 9, (CC) dc 1, (MC) dc 1, (CC) dc 1, (MC) dc 2, (CC) dc 1, (MC) dc 4, (CC) dc 1, (MC) dc 4, (CC) dc 1, (MC) dc 1, (CC) dc 1, (MC) dc 1, (CC) dc 1, (MC) dc 13, (CC) dc 1, (MC) dc 6, (CC) dc 1, (MC) dc 6, (CC) dc 1, (MC) dc 5. [143 sts]

**Row 74:** (MC) ch 2, turn, dc 5, (CC) dc 1, (MC) dc 6, (CC) dc 1, (MC) dc 6, (CC) dc 1, (MC) dc 13, (CC) dc 1, (MC) dc 1, (CC) dc 1, (MC) dc 2, (CC) dc 1, (MC) dc 5, (CC) dc 1, (MC) dc 5, (CC) dc 1, (MC) dc 1, (CC) dc 1, (MC) dc 8, (CC) dc 1, (MC) dc 3, (CC) dc 1, (MC) dc 2, (CC) dc 1, (MC) dc 5, (CC) dc 1, (MC) dc 1, (CC) dc 1, (MC) dc 1, (CC) dc 1, (MC) dc 2, (CC) dc 1, (MC) dc 8, (CC) dc 1, (MC) dc 1, (CC) dc 1, (MC) dc 5, (CC) dc 1, (MC) dc 5, (CC) dc 1, (MC) dc 2, (CC) dc 1, (MC) dc 1, (CC) dc 1, (MC) dc 13, (CC) dc 1, (MC) dc 6, (CC) dc 1, (MC) dc 6, (CC) dc 1, (MC) dc 5. [143 sts]

**Row 75:** (MC) ch 2, turn, dc 4, (CC) dc 1, (MC) dc 1, (CC) dc 2, (MC) dc 3, (CC) dc 3, (MC) dc 3, (CC) dc 2, (MC) dc 1, (CC) dc 1, (MC) dc 12, (CC) dc 1, (MC) dc 2, (CC) dc 1, (MC) dc 3, (CC) dc 1, (MC) dc 9, (CC) dc 1, (MC) dc 1, (CC) dc 1, (MC) dc 8, (CC) dc 1, (MC) dc 7, (CC) dc 1, (MC) dc 3, (CC) dc 1, (MC) dc 5, (CC) dc 1, (MC) dc 1, (CC) dc 1, (MC) dc 8, (CC) dc 1, (MC) dc 1, (CC) dc 1, (MC) dc 9, (CC) dc 1, (MC) dc 3, (CC) dc 1, (MC) dc 2, (CC) dc 1, (MC) dc 12, (CC) dc 1, (MC) dc 1, (CC) dc 2, (MC) dc 3, (CC) dc 3, (MC) dc 3, (CC) dc 2, (MC) dc 1, (CC) dc 1, (MC) dc 4. [143 sts]

**Row 76:** (MC) ch 2, turn, dc 3, (CC) dc 1, (MC) dc 4, (CC) dc 1, (MC) dc 1, (CC) dc 2, (MC) dc 1, (CC) dc 2, (MC) dc 1, (CC) dc 1, (MC) dc 4, (CC) dc 1, (MC) dc 12, (CC) dc 1, (MC) dc 2, (CC) dc 1, (MC) dc 5, (CC) dc 1, (MC) dc 2, (CC) dc 1, (MC) dc 3, (CC) dc 1, (MC) dc 1, (CC) dc 1, (MC) dc 8, (CC) dc 1, (MC) dc 3, (CC) dc 1, (MC) dc 1, (CC) dc 1, (MC) dc 2, (CC) dc 1, (MC) dc 1, (CC) dc 1, (MC) dc 2, (CC) dc 1, (MC) dc 1, (CC) dc 1, (MC) dc 1, (CC) dc 1, (MC) dc 1, (CC) dc 1, (MC) dc 8, (CC) dc 1, (MC) dc 1, (CC) dc 1, (MC) dc 3, (CC) dc 1, (MC) dc 2, (CC) dc 1, (MC) dc 5, (CC) dc 1, (MC) dc 2, (CC) dc 1, (MC) dc 12, (CC) dc 1, (MC) dc 4, (CC) dc 1, (MC) dc 1, (CC) dc 2, (MC) dc 1, (CC) dc 2, (MC) dc 1, (CC) dc 1, (MC) dc 4, (CC) dc 1, (MC) dc 3. [143 sts]

**Row 77:** (MC) ch 2, turn, dc 3, (CC) dc 1, (MC) dc 5, (CC) dc 2, (MC) dc 3, (CC) dc 2, (MC) dc 5, (CC) dc 1, (MC) dc 13, (CC) dc 1, (MC) dc 2, (CC) dc 1, (MC) dc 5, (CC) dc 1, (MC) dc 4, (CC) dc 1, (MC) dc 1, (CC) dc 2, (MC) dc 8, (CC) dc 1, (MC) dc 2, (CC) dc 1, (MC) dc 4, (CC) dc 2, (MC) dc 1, (CC) dc 2, (MC) dc 4, (CC) dc 1, (MC) dc 2, (CC) dc 1, (MC) dc 8, (CC) dc 2, (MC) dc 1, (CC) dc 1, (MC) dc 4, (CC) dc 1, (MC) dc 5, (CC) dc 1, (MC) dc 2, (CC) dc 1, (MC) dc 13, (CC) dc 1, (MC) dc 5, (CC) dc 2, (MC) dc 3, (CC) dc 2, (MC) dc 5, (CC) dc 1, (MC) dc 3. [143 sts]

**Row 78:** (MC) ch 2, turn, dc 4, (CC) dc 1, (MC) dc 5, (CC) dc 1, (MC) dc 3, (CC) dc 1, (MC) dc 5, (CC) dc 1, (MC) dc 15, (CC) dc 1, (MC) dc 2, (CC) dc 1, (MC) dc 8, (CC) dc 1, (MC) dc 2, (CC) dc 1, (MC) dc 10, (CC) dc 1, (MC) dc 2, (CC) dc 1, (MC) dc 1, (CC) dc 1, (MC) dc 2, (CC) dc 1, (MC) dc 1, (CC) dc 1, (MC) dc 3, (CC) dc 1, (MC) dc 3, (CC) dc 1, (MC) dc 10, (CC) dc 1, (MC) dc 2, (CC) dc 1, (MC) dc 8, (CC) dc 1, (MC) dc 2, (CC) dc 1, (MC) dc 15, (CC) dc 1, (MC) dc 5, (CC) dc 1, (MC) dc 3, (CC) dc 1, (MC) dc 5, (CC) dc 1, (MC) dc 4. [143 sts]

**Row 79:** (MC) ch 2, turn, dc 3, (CC) dc 1, (MC) dc 5, (CC) dc 2, (MC) dc 3, (CC) dc 2, (MC) dc 5, (CC) dc 1, (MC) dc 15, (CC) dc 1, (MC) dc 2, (CC) dc 8, (MC) dc 2, (CC) dc 1, (MC) dc 12, (CC) dc 1, (MC) dc 5, (CC) dc 1, (MC) dc 3, (CC) dc 1, (MC) dc 5, (CC) dc 1, (MC) dc 12, (CC) dc 1, (MC) dc 2, (CC) dc 8, (MC) dc 2, (CC) dc 1, (MC) dc 15, (CC) dc 1, (MC) dc 5, (CC) dc 2, (MC) dc 3, (CC) dc 2, (MC) dc 5, (CC) dc 1, (MC) dc 3. [143 sts]

**Row 80:** (MC) ch 2, turn, dc 3, (CC) dc 1, (MC) dc 4, (CC) dc 1, (MC) dc 1, (CC) dc 2, (MC) dc 1, (CC) dc 2, (MC) dc 1, (CC) dc 1, (MC) dc 4, (CC) dc 1, (MC) dc 16, (CC) dc 2, (MC) dc 9, (CC) dc 1, (MC) dc 14, (CC) dc 5, (MC) dc 5, (CC) dc 5, (MC) dc 14, (CC) dc 1, (MC) dc 9, (CC) dc 2, (MC) dc 16, (CC) dc 1, (MC) dc 4, (CC) dc 1, (MC) dc 1, (CC) dc 2, (MC) dc 1, (CC) dc 2, (MC) dc 1, (CC) dc 1, (MC) dc 4, (CC) dc 1, (MC) dc 3. [143 sts]

**Row 81:** (MC) ch 2, turn, dc 4, (CC) dc 1, (MC) dc 1, (CC) dc 2, (MC) dc 3, (CC) dc 3, (MC) dc 3, (CC) dc 2, (MC) dc 1, (CC) dc 1, (MC) dc 18, (CC) dc 10, (MC) dc 45, (CC) dc 10, (MC) dc 18, (CC) dc 1, (MC) dc 1, (CC) dc 2, (MC) dc 3, (CC) dc 3, (MC) dc 3, (CC) dc 2, (MC) dc 1, (CC) dc 1, (MC) dc 4. [143 sts]

**Row 82:** (MC) ch 2, turn, dc 5, (CC) dc 1, (MC) dc 6, (CC) dc 1, (MC) dc 6, (CC) dc 1, (MC) dc 3, (CC) dc 1, (MC) dc 5, (CC) dc 1, (MC) dc 5, (CC) dc 1, (MC) dc 5, (CC) dc 1, (MC) dc 5, (CC) dc 1, (MC) dc 5, (CC) dc 1, (MC) dc 5, (CC) dc 1, (MC) dc 5, (CC) dc 1, (MC) dc 5, (CC) dc 1, (MC) dc 5, (CC) dc 1, (MC) dc 5, (CC) dc 1, (MC) dc 5, (CC) dc 1, (MC) dc 5, (CC) dc 1, (MC) dc 5, (CC) dc 1, (MC) dc 3, (CC) dc 1, (MC) dc 6, (CC) dc 1, (MC) dc 6, (CC) dc 1, (MC) dc 5. [143 sts]

# Flower Paisley Blanket (Continued)

**Row 83:** (MC) ch 2, turn, dc 5, (CC) dc 1, (MC) dc 6, (CC) dc 1, (MC) dc 6, (CC) dc 1, (MC) dc 3, (CC) dc 1, (MC) dc 5, (CC) dc 1, (MC) dc 5, (CC) dc 1, (MC) dc 5, (CC) dc 1, (MC) dc 5, (CC) dc 1, (MC) dc 5, (CC) dc 1, (MC) dc 5, (CC) dc 1, (MC) dc 5, (CC) dc 1, (MC) dc 5, (CC) dc 1, (MC) dc 5, (CC) dc 1, (MC) dc 5, (CC) dc 1, (MC) dc 5, (CC) dc 1, (MC) dc 5, (CC) dc 1, (MC) dc 5, (CC) dc 1, (MC) dc 5, (CC) dc 1, (MC) dc 5, (CC) dc 1, (MC) dc 5, (CC) dc 1, (MC) dc 3, (CC) dc 1, (MC) dc 6, (CC) dc 1, (MC) dc 6, (CC) dc 1, (MC) dc 5. [143 sts]

**Row 84:** (MC) ch 2, turn, dc 6, (CC) dc 1, (MC) dc 5, (CC) dc 1, (MC) dc 5, (CC) dc 1, (MC) dc 7, (CC) dc 1, (MC) dc 5, (CC) dc 1, (MC) dc 5, (CC) dc 1, (MC) dc 5, (CC) dc 1, (MC) dc 5, (CC) dc 1, (MC) dc 5, (CC) dc 1, (MC) dc 5, (CC) dc 1, (MC) dc 5, (CC) dc 1, (MC) dc 5, (CC) dc 1, (MC) dc 5, (CC) dc 1, (MC) dc 5, (CC) dc 1, (MC) dc 5, (CC) dc 1, (MC) dc 5, (CC) dc 1, (MC) dc 5, (CC) dc 1, (MC) dc 7, (CC) dc 1, (MC) dc 5, (CC) dc 1, (MC) dc 5, (CC) dc 1, (MC) dc 6. [143 sts]

**Row 85:** (MC) ch 2, turn, dc 7, (CC) dc 2, (MC) dc 2, (CC) dc 1, (MC) dc 1, (CC) dc 1, (MC) dc 3, (CC) dc 1, (MC) dc 7, (CC) dc 3, (MC) dc 3, (CC) dc 3, (MC) dc 3, (CC) dc 3, (MC) dc 3, (CC) dc 3, (MC) dc 3, (CC) dc 3, (MC) dc 3, (CC) dc 3, (MC) dc 3, (CC) dc 3, (MC) dc 3, (CC) dc 3, (MC) dc 3, (CC) dc 3, (MC) dc 3, (CC) dc 3, (MC) dc 3, (CC) dc 3, (MC) dc 3, (CC) dc 3, (MC) dc 3, (CC) dc 3, (MC) dc 3, (CC) dc 3, (MC) dc 3, (CC) dc 3, (MC) dc 7, (CC) dc 2, (MC) dc 2, (CC) dc 1, (MC) dc 1, (CC) dc 1, (MC) dc 3, (CC) dc 1, (MC) dc 7. [143 sts]

**Row 86:** (MC) ch 2, turn, dc 8, (CC) dc 3, (MC) dc 3, (CC) dc 3, (MC) dc 9, (CC) dc 1, (MC) dc 5, (CC) dc 1, (MC) dc 5, (CC) dc 1, (MC) dc 5, (CC) dc 1, (MC) dc 5, (CC) dc 1, (MC) dc 5, (CC) dc 1, (MC) dc 5, (CC) dc 1, (MC) dc 5, (CC) dc 1, (MC) dc 5, (CC) dc 1, (MC) dc 5, (CC) dc 1, (MC) dc 5, (CC) dc 1, (MC) dc 5, (CC) dc 1, (MC) dc 5, (CC) dc 1, (MC) dc 5, (CC) dc 1, (MC) dc 5, (CC) dc 1, (MC) dc 9, (CC) dc 3, (MC) dc 3, (CC) dc 3, (MC) dc 8. [143 sts]

Fasten off the CC, and continue using the the MC for the last few rows.

**Rows 87 through 90:** (MC) ch 2, turn, dc across. [143 sts]

Fasten off and weave in all the ends.

# Charts

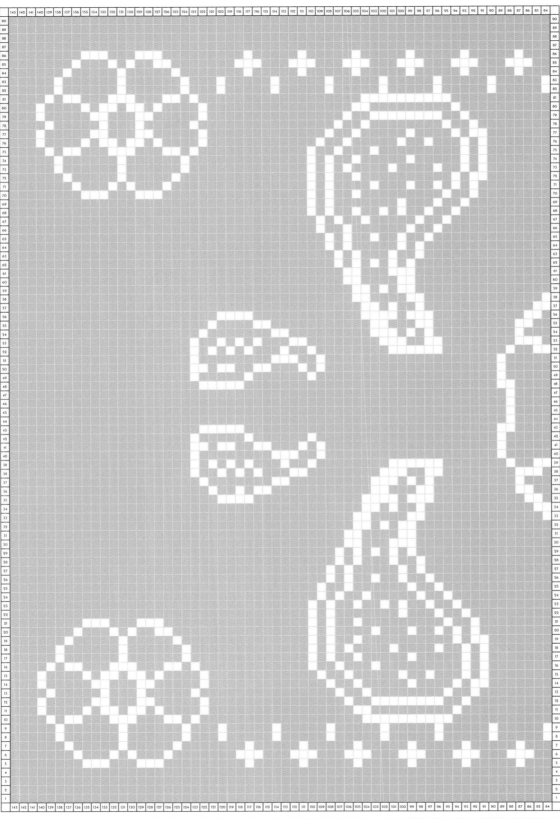

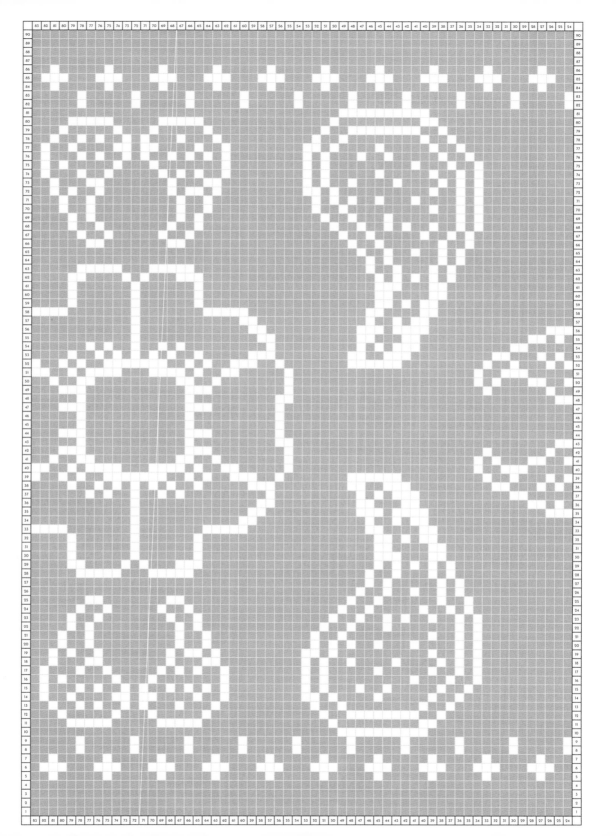

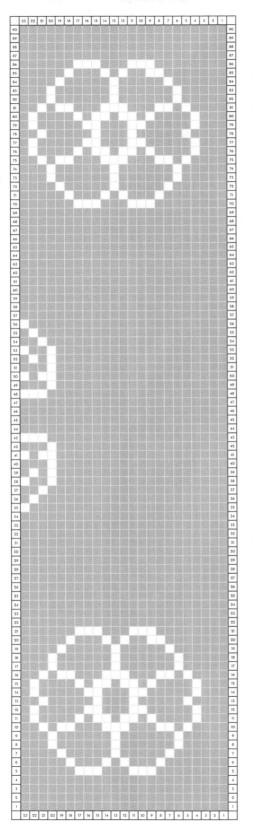

Main Color

Contrast Color

For chart notes and how to read a chart, see pages 15-17.

# Intarsia Crochet

If you're ready to create wearable artwork, then you are going to love intarsia crochet. Intarsia crochet is the crochet colorwork technique that involves lots of colors without having them carried through each stitch. With this technique, you can add an endless number of colors! You can create everything from intricate crochet photos on your designs, or add pops of color on your projects without it being on the entire design.

Intarsia crochet centers around joining small bits of yarn, called bobbins, at each point that you need them. This way, the colors aren't carried throughout the project, which creates a cleaner overall design. It also allows for more intricate designs to be created. If you want to make realistic or bold artwork on your crochet patterns, you will love this technique. It is also helpful when you are using highly contrasting colors and want to just have the contrasting color at the point where you need it. Or you can use it when your colorwork is spaced far apart.

I love using intarsia crochet to create very intricate designs. I am a huge fan of adding nature motifs to my designs in the forms of flowers or animals. Sometimes they just consist of one color with the colorwork far apart, or I use five or more colors to get a detailed recreation of a flower. Intarsia crochet really allows you to let your imagination run wild and create a colorwork design that captures just what you want!

In this chapter, I'll be walking you through all of the basics of intarsia crochet. From how to use bobbins, joining the colors, working it flat and in the round and more, you'll learn everything you need to know to get started. You'll learn how to do the basics of the technique with the Homestead Pillow (page 79) and how to create more intricate pictures with the Bloom Sweater (page 99).

# Basic Intarsia Crochet Techniques

### How to Do Intarsia Crochet Worked Flat and in the Round

Just like tapestry crochet, intarsia crochet is worked differently when it's worked flat and in the round. Since you join the colors at each point where you need them, that changes how each project is worked. Here are some tips:

#### Worked Flat

Intarsia crochet is often easier to do when it's worked flat instead of in the round, from keeping track of your bobbins to preventing them from tangling.

**Using Bobbins:** When you do intarsia worked flat, you will work it back and forth like a normal flat crochet piece, but instead you'll have bobbins to manage. Bobbins will be joined at each point you need a new color, and you can place them on a stand or holder (like a pasta drying rack) to prevent them from tangling.

**Keeping Proper Tension:** Since you will be changing colors more often with intarsia crochet, you'll want to make sure that you pull the stitches closed when you switch colors. When you work the piece flat, this can be especially noticeable when your tension is too loose because there will be holes where color changes happened (see photo 1). When working on the right side, you can pull the stitch closed (see photo 2). When working on the wrong side, I find that crossing the color I'm switching from over the one I'm switching to helps close the holes better.

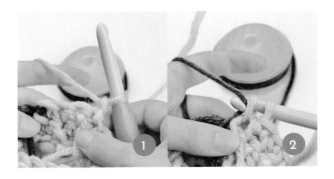

## Worked in the Round

**Using Bobbins:** When you do intarsia crochet in the round, it's very different from tapestry crochet (page 23). Instead of working in continuous rounds, you will turn each round (see photo 1 above). This means you do not have to carry each bobbin or rejoin new ones on each round (see photo 2). Instead, you're able to turn and work back to the points where you just ended with one bobbin and use it again.

**Offsetting Slanting:** Just like tapestry crochet (page 23), you'll only work in certain loops when crocheting in the round to help prevent the stitches from slanting. When you work on the right side, you'll do your stitches in the back loops only (see photo 1). On the wrong side, you'll do your stitches through the front loops only (see photo 2). This creates a very similar look to working in the back loops only for the entire project as in tapestry crochet.

## Using Yarn Bobbins

You might be wondering, "What is a yarn bobbin?" A yarn bobbin is a small amount of yarn in the form of a ball or wound around a small item such as a clothespin. Yarn bobbins help you to join small amounts of a color at different points in your project without needing to carry it or using a large amount of yarn.

If you'll be using a yarn bobbin in your project, you'll start by looking at the chart and pattern you'll be making to plan out how many you'll need. You'll need a bobbin for each point you will be switching colors. However, if there are just one or two stitches between two colors, then you don't need to join a yarn bobbin every other stitch. Just carry the yarn for those few stitches, and then join a bobbin on the next large color change.

To make a yarn bobbin, you can wind small balls of yarn, or you can wind your yarn around an item like a clothespin. If you wind it to a clothespin, then you can organize the colors more easily by clipping them to a basket or edge of something else that you can easily move them around on. Within the pattern, it will list an approximate yardage amount needed for each color, and you can use a yardstick or tape measure to make sure you have the right amount you need for each bobbin.

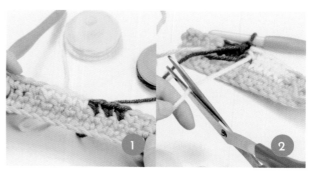

## Joining New Colors

- **Add a color:** When you are joining a new color, that is when you will add in a new bobbin to your project (see photo 1 above). You'll use a separate bobbin for each color that you are using, and/or for each point you will be changing colors (see photo 2).

- **Finish using a bobbin:** Once you have all of your yarn bobbins joined, you will use them throughout the rest of your project. Use each bobbin until you do all of the stitches needed to get to the next one, then leave that yarn until you need it in the next row (see photo 1). After you have done all of the stitches for that specific bobbin, fasten it off since you won't need it any longer (see photo 2).

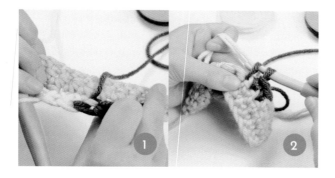

- **Take it or leave it:** Whenever you join a new color, instead of carrying the unused yarn, you will leave it at the last stitch you did with it (see photo 1). Then you use the new color until you get to the point where there is a color change or new color (see photo 2).

*The Homestead Pillow is inspired by the brightly colored houses that lie in the older districts of San Francisco. I love how those homes have so many different colors, and I thought a pillow of them would look amazing! This is our first intarsia crochet project of this book, and it will help you dive right into the technique. You'll learn how to use bobbins instead of carrying each color, and really see how many colors you can use. It also will teach you how to combine both intarsia and tapestry crochet.*

# Homestead Pillow

## Pattern Level: Beginner

**Gauge:** 4" x 4" (10 x 10 cm) square = 14 hdc x 12 rows

**Dimensions:** 26" x 17" (66 x 43 cm) (fits a 26" x 17" [66 x 43-cm] pillow form)

**Hook:** US H/8 5mm

**Yarn:** Lion Brand Basic Stitch Premium (Yarn Weight 4 Medium, 219 yds [200 m], 3.5 oz [100 g], 100 percent acrylic) in four colors:
- White (MC)
- Saffron (CC1)
- Boysenberry (CC3)
- Plum (CC5)

Lion Brand Basic Stitch Anti-Pilling (Yarn Weight 4 Medium, 185 yds [170 m], 3.5 oz [100 g], 100 percent acrylic) in three colors:
- Blue/White (CC2)
- Prism (CC4)
- Tan/White (CC6)

**Approximate Yarn Yardage:**

MC = 555 yds (507 m)
CC1 = 50 yds (46 m)
CC2 = 25 yds (23 m)
CC3 = 50 yds (46 m)
CC4 = 25 yds (23 m)
CC5 = 50 yds (46 m)
CC6 = 25 yds (23 m)

**Extra Materials:**

Yarn needle

**Abbreviations:**

ch = chain
hdc = half double crochet
st(s) = stitch(es)
MC = main color
CC1 = contrast color 1
CC2 = contrast color 2
CC3 = contrast color 3
CC4 = contrast color 4
CC5 = contrast color 5
CC6 = contrast color 6

# Homestead Pillow (Continued)

## Front Panel

Starting with MC, ch 92.

**Row 1:** starting in third ch from hook, hdc 90.

**Rows 2 through 12:** ch 2 (ch 2 at the beginning of the row does not count as a st throughout the rest of the pattern), turn, hdc across. [90 sts]

We'll now begin adding in the colors for the different houses. Since we are using intarsia crochet for this, create a bobbin for each point at which you are adding a new color. For each house, you will make 3 bobbins: 2 for the main part of the house, and 1 for the door. Then you'll also make a bobbin for the portion of the main color between the houses.

**Row 13:** (MC) ch 2, turn, hdc 12, add bobbin of (CC1) and hdc 5, add bobbin of (CC2) and hdc 5 (see photo above), add bobbin of (CC1) and hdc 5, (MC) hdc 10, add bobbin of (CC3) and hdc 5, add bobbin of (CC4) and hdc 5, add bobbin of (CC3) and hdc 5, (MC) hdc 10, add bobbin of (CC5) and hdc 5, add bobbin of (CC6) and hdc 5, add bobbin of (CC5) and hdc 5, (MC) hdc 13. [90 sts]

**Row 14:** (MC) ch 2, turn, hdc 13, (CC5) hdc 5, (CC6) hdc 5, (CC5) hdc 5, (MC) hdc 10, (CC3) hdc 5, (CC4) hdc 5, (CC3) hdc 5, (MC) hdc 10, (CC1) hdc 5, (CC2) hdc 5, (CC1) hdc 5, (MC) hdc 12. [90 sts]

**Row 15:** (MC) ch 2, turn, hdc 12, (CC1) hdc 5, (CC2) hdc 5, (CC1) hdc 5, (MC) hdc 10, (CC3) hdc 5, (CC4) hdc 5, (CC3) hdc 5, (MC) hdc 10, (CC5) hdc 5, (CC6) hdc 5, (CC5) hdc 5, (MC) hdc 13. [90 sts]

In this next row, there will be single stitches on the doors. You do not need to create a separate bobbin for those. Instead, carry the main house color to that stitch, and do the single stitch with the carried yarn.

**Row 16:** (MC) ch 2, turn, hdc 13, (CC5) hdc 5, (CC6) hdc 1, (CC5) hdc 1, (CC6) hdc 3, (CC5) hdc 5, (MC) hdc 10, (CC3) hdc 5, (CC4) hdc 1, (CC3) hdc 1, (CC4) hdc 3, (CC3) hdc 5, (MC) hdc 10, (CC1) hdc 5, (CC2) hdc 1, (CC1) hdc 1, (CC2) hdc 3, (CC1) hdc 5, (MC) hdc 12. [90 sts]

**Row 17:** (MC) ch 2, turn, hdc 12, (CC1) hdc 5, (CC2) hdc 5, (CC1) hdc 5, (MC) hdc 10, (CC3) hdc 5, (CC4) hdc 5, (CC3) hdc 5, (MC) hdc 10, (CC5) hdc 5, (CC6) hdc 5, (CC5) hdc 5, (MC) hdc 13. [90 sts]

**Row 18:** (MC) ch 2, turn, hdc 13, (CC5) hdc 5, (CC6) hdc 5, (CC5) hdc 5, (MC) hdc 10, (CC3) hdc 5, (CC4) hdc 5, (CC3) hdc 5, (MC) hdc 10, (CC1) hdc 5, (CC2) hdc 5, (CC1) hdc 5, (MC) hdc 12. [90 sts]

**Row 19:** (MC) ch 2, turn, hdc 12, (CC1) hdc 5, (CC2) hdc 5, (CC1) hdc 5, (MC) hdc 10, (CC3) hdc 5, (CC4) hdc 5, (CC3) hdc 5, (MC) hdc 10, (CC5) hdc 5, (CC6) hdc 5, (CC5) hdc 5, (MC) hdc 13. [90 sts]

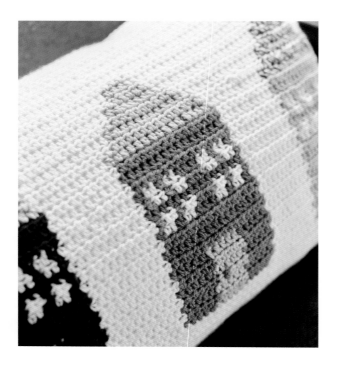

Fasten off CC2, CC4 and CC6. We will join them again when we start the roofs.

**Row 20:** (MC) ch 2, turn, hdc 13, (CC5) hdc 15, (MC) hdc 10, (CC3) hdc 15, (MC) hdc 10, (CC1) hdc 15, (MC) hdc 12. [90 sts]

**Row 21:** (MC) ch 2, turn, hdc 12, (CC1) hdc 15, (MC) hdc 10, (CC3) hdc 15, (MC) hdc 10, (CC5) hdc 15, (MC) hdc 13. [90 sts]

**Row 22:** (MC) ch 2, turn, hdc 13, (CC5) hdc 15, (MC) hdc 10, (CC3) hdc 15, (MC) hdc 10, (CC1) hdc 15, (MC) hdc 12. [90 sts]

Now that we will begin doing the windows, for the next two rows, we will combine the two techniques we know so far: tapestry and intarsia crochet. Since the windows are a small amount of sts before you switch colors, it can get tedious and frustrating to have so many bobbins at each color change. In comes tapestry crochet (see page 24 for how to do this technique)! While you are working the next two rows, you will not pick up the bobbins of MC between the houses. Instead, you will use the MC from the start of the row, across each house and between houses, all the way to the end of the row. Don't fasten off your MC bobbins; we will use them soon.

**Row 23:** (MC) ch 2, turn, hdc 12, (CC1) hdc 1, (MC) hdc 2, (CC1) hdc 1 (see above photo for using the MC again), (MC) hdc 2, (CC1) hdc 3, (MC) hdc 2, (CC1) hdc 1, (MC) hdc 2, (CC1) hdc 1, (MC) hdc 10, (CC3) hdc 1, (MC) hdc 2, (CC3) hdc 1, (MC) hdc 2, (CC3) hdc 3, (MC) hdc 2, (CC3) hdc 1, (MC) hdc 2, (CC3) hdc 1, (MC) hdc 10, (CC5) hdc 1, (MC) hdc 2, (CC5) hdc 1, (MC) hdc 2, (CC5) hdc 3, (MC) hdc 2, (CC5) hdc 1, (MC) hdc 2, (CC5) hdc 1, (MC) hdc 13. [90 sts]

Row 24: (MC) ch 2, turn, hdc 13, (CC5) hdc 1, (MC) hdc 2, (CC5) hdc 1, (MC) hdc 2, (CC5) hdc 3, (MC) hdc 2, (CC5) hdc 1, (MC) hdc 2, (CC5) hdc 1, (MC) hdc 10, (CC3) hdc 1, (MC) hdc 2, (CC3) hdc 1, (MC) hdc 2, (CC3) hdc 3, (MC) hdc 2, (CC3) hdc 1, (MC) hdc 2, (CC3) hdc 1, (MC) hdc 10, (CC1) hdc 1, (MC) hdc 2, (CC1) hdc 1, (MC) hdc 2, (CC1) hdc 3, (MC) hdc 2, (CC1) hdc 1, (MC) hdc 2, (CC1) hdc 1, (MC) hdc 12. [90 sts]

For the next row, use the MC bobbins in between the houses again.

Row 25: (MC) ch 2, turn, hdc 12, (CC1) hdc 15, (MC) hdc 10, (CC3) hdc 15, (MC) hdc 10, (CC5) hdc 15, (MC) hdc 13. [90 sts]

For the next two rows, carry your yarn like you did in rows 23 and 24.

Row 26: (MC) ch 2, turn, hdc 13, (CC5) hdc 1, (MC) hdc 2, (CC5) hdc 1, (MC) hdc 2, (CC5) hdc 3, (MC) hdc 2, (CC5) hdc 1, (MC) hdc 2, (CC5) hdc 1, (MC) hdc 10, (CC3) hdc 1, (MC) hdc 2, (CC3) hdc 1, (MC) hdc 2, (CC3) hdc 3, (MC) hdc 2, (CC3) hdc 1, (MC) hdc 2, (CC3) hdc 1, (MC) hdc 10, (CC1) hdc 1, (MC) hdc 2, (CC1) hdc 1, (MC) hdc 2, (CC1) hdc 3, (MC) hdc 2, (CC1) hdc 1, (MC) hdc 2, (CC1) hdc 1, (MC) hdc 12. [90 sts]

Row 27: (MC) ch 2, turn, hdc 12, (CC1) hdc 1, (MC) hdc 2, (CC1) hdc 1, (MC) hdc 2, (CC1) hdc 3, (MC) hdc 2, (CC1) hdc 1, (MC) hdc 2, (CC1) hdc 1, (MC) hdc 10, (CC3) hdc 1, (MC) hdc 2, (CC3) hdc 1, (MC) hdc 2, (CC3) hdc 3, (MC) hdc 2, (CC3) hdc 1, (MC) hdc 2, (CC3) hdc 1, (MC) hdc 10, (CC5) hdc 1, (MC) hdc 2, (CC5) hdc 1, (MC) hdc 2, (CC5) hdc 3, (MC) hdc 2, (CC5) hdc 1, (MC) hdc 2, (CC5) hdc 1, (MC) hdc 13. [90 sts]

Now, you'll resume using the bobbins for the houses in this next row, and throughout the rest of the pattern, unless it says to fasten off for a certain color.

Row 28: (MC) ch 2, turn, hdc 13, (CC5) hdc 15, (MC) hdc 10, (CC3) hdc 15, (MC) hdc 10, (CC1) hdc 15, (MC) hdc 12. [90 sts]

Row 29: (MC) ch 2, turn, hdc 12, (CC1) hdc 15, (MC) hdc 10, (CC3) hdc 15, (MC) hdc 10, (CC5) hdc 15, (MC) hdc 13. [90 sts]

Row 30: (MC) ch 2, turn, hdc 13, (CC5) hdc 15, (MC) hdc 10, (CC3) hdc 15, (MC) hdc 10, (CC1) hdc 15, (MC) hdc 12. [90 sts]

Fasten off CC1, CC3 and CC5. You'll add in CC2, CC4 and CC6 again to make the roofs of the houses.

Row 31: (MC) ch 2, turn, hdc 12, (CC2) hdc 15, (MC) hdc 10, (CC4) hdc 15, (MC) hdc 10, (CC6) hdc 15, (MC) hdc 13. [90 sts]

Row 32: (MC) ch 2, turn, hdc 14, (CC6) hdc 13, (MC) hdc 12, (CC4) hdc 13, (MC) hdc 12, (CC2) hdc 13, (MC) hdc 13. [90 sts]

Row 33: (MC) ch 2, turn, hdc 14, (CC2) hdc 11, (MC) hdc 14, (CC4) hdc 11, (MC) hdc 14, (CC6) hdc 11, (MC) hdc 15. [90 sts]

Row 34: (MC) ch 2, turn, hdc 16, (CC6) hdc 9, (MC) hdc 16, (CC4) hdc 9, (MC) hdc 16, (CC2) hdc 9, (MC) hdc 15. [90 sts]

Row 35: (MC) ch 2, turn, hdc 16, (CC2) hdc 7, (MC) hdc 18, (CC4) hdc 7, (MC) hdc 18, (CC6) hdc 7, (MC) hdc 17. [90 sts]

Row 36: (MC) ch 2, turn, hdc 18, (CC6) hdc 5, (MC) hdc 20, (CC4) hdc 5, (MC) hdc 20, (CC2) hdc 5, (MC) hdc 17. [90 sts]

**Row 37:** (MC) ch 2, turn, hdc 18, (CC2) hdc 3, (MC) hdc 22, (CC4) hdc 3, (MC) hdc 22, (CC6) hdc 3, (MC) hdc 19. [90 sts]

**Row 38:** (MC) ch 2, turn, hdc 20, (CC6) hdc 1, (MC) hdc 24, (CC4) hdc 1, (MC) hdc 24, (CC2) hdc 1, (MC) hdc 19. [90 sts]

Fasten off CC2, CC4 and CC6, as well as all the MC bobbins except the one that finished the last row.

**Rows 39 through 50:** (MC) ch 2, turn, hdc across. [90 sts]

Fasten off MC, and weave in the ends.

## Back Panel

Starting with MC, ch 92.

**Row 1:** starting in third ch from hook, hdc 90.

**Rows 2 through 50:** ch 2, turn, hdc across. [90 sts]

Fasten off MC, and weave in the ends.

## Assembly

Once panels are both finished, it's time to assemble them. Take a 16″ x 24″ (40.5 x 61-cm) pillow form to sew the panels around. You can start assembling the panels before inserting the pillow form, or assemble them around the pillow at the start.

If you are doing it around the pillow form, take both panels and position them on the sides you'd prefer. Pin them together, and then seam together along the edges using your favorite seaming method (see pages 18-21). I recommend using the mattress stitch (page 19) when doing it around the pillow form.

If you are assembling the panels by themselves, put the right sides together, pin and seam along the two short sides as well as the top. See pages 18-21 for different seaming methods. I recommend using either a slip stitch seam (page 21) or the mattress stitch (page 19). Once you have those three sides seamed, turn right sides out and fit around the pillow form. Pin the bottom edges together, and seam together using the mattress stitch.

Once you are finished seaming, fasten off and weave in the ends.

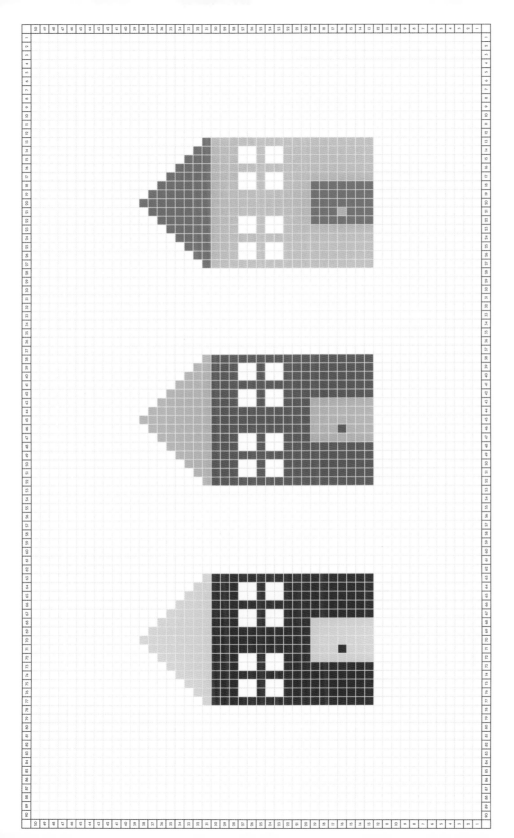

## Chart

☐ Main Color

▨ Contrast Color 1

▨ Contrast Color 2

▨ Contrast Color 3

▨ Contrast Color 4

■ Contrast Color 5

▧ Contrast Color 6

For chart notes and
how to read a chart, see
pages 15–17.

*The Wanderer Beanie is inspired by adventures into the unknown, where you let your feet take you where they want to go. The arrows point to any direction and create such a beautiful hat! This beanie pattern will teach you how to do intarsia crochet in the round, using some of the same techniques we used for the Queen of Diamonds Hat in the previous chapter (see pages 32-35).*

# Wanderer Beanie

## Pattern Level: Intermediate

**Gauge:** 4″ x 4″ (10 x 10 cm) square = 14 hdc x 9 rows

**Finished Hat Measurements:**
- Circumference: 21″ (53 cm) around
- Hat Height: 8″ (20 cm)

**Hook:** US J/10 6mm

**Yarn:** Lion Brand Heartland (Yarn Weight 4 Medium, 251 yds [230 m], 5 oz [142 g], 100 percent acrylic) in 2 to 3 colors (Pattern can be done with 2 colors, or 3 colors as shown in the sample. The third color is optional.):
- Kings Canyon (MC)
- Yosemite (CC1)
- Yellowstone (if using a second contrast color, then it is CC2)

**Approximate Yarn Yardage:**

MC = 100 yds (92 m)

CC1 = 70 yds (64 m)

CC2 (optional if using second color) = 70 yds (64 m)

**Extra Materials:**

Yarn needle

**Abbreviations:**

ch = chain

hdc = half double crochet

st(s) = stitch(es)

sl st = slip stitch

rnd = round

blo = back loops only

flo = front loops only

MC = main color

CC1 = contrast color 1

CC2 = contrast color 2 (if using)

## Chart

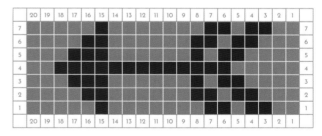

Main Color

Contrast Color

For chart notes and how to read a chart, see pages 15-17. Same chart used for CC1 and CC2.

# Wanderer Beanie (Continued)

## Brim

Starting with CC1, ch 8.

**Row 1:** starting in third ch from hook, hdc 6.

**Row 2:** ch 2 (ch 2 at the beginning of the row does not count as a st throughout the rest of the pattern), turn, hdc across in the blo.

**Row 3:** ch 2, turn, hdc across in the flo.

For the next 37 rows, alternate between repeating rows 2 and 3.

Once you're done with those rows, join the two ends of your brim right sides together with a sl st. Turn it right-side out, and then you'll move on to the body of the hat.

## Body of Hat

Fasten off CC1, and join the MC by using it to do the first ch 1. To start the hat, we'll begin by doing a base layer of hdc that we'll build the rest of the hat on.

**Rnd 1:** ch 1 (ch 1 at the beginning of the rnd does not count as a st throughout the rest of the pattern), hdc 76 around the top of the brim of the beanie, which is slightly less than 2 sts per brim row, join with sl st to ch 1 at beginning of rnd. [76 sts]

The next rnd will begin the colorwork for the hat. Create a bobbin for each color of arrow. I used two colors for my arrows, but you could easily just do one or even more if you'd like. Since we are starting the colorwork, we will also be starting to alternate between crocheting in the blo and flo to help offset any slanting from crocheting in the rnd. All even rows will be blo, and all odd rows will be flo.

**Rnd 2 (blo):** starting with the MC, ch 1, *hdc 2, (CC1) hdc 2, (MC) hdc 1, (CC1) hdc 2, (MC) hdc 7, (CC1) hdc 1, (MC) hdc 5, repeat from * 3 more times, to create the multicolored arrows alternate between CC1 and CC2 for each arrow, join with sl st to ch 2 at beginning of rnd. [76 sts]

**Rnd 3 (flo):** (MC) ch 2, turn, *hdc 4, (CC1) hdc 2, (MC) hdc 6, (CC1) hdc 2, (MC) hdc 1, (CC1) hdc 2, (MC) hdc 3, repeat from * 3 more times, join with sl st to ch 2 at beginning of rnd. [76 sts]

**Rnd 4 (blo):** (MC) ch 2, turn, *hdc 4, (CC1) hdc 2, (MC) hdc 1, (CC1) hdc 1, (MC) hdc 6, (CC1) hdc 3, (MC) hdc 3, repeat from * 3 more times, join with sl st to ch 2 at beginning of rnd. [76 sts]

**Rnd 5 (flo):** (MC) ch 2, turn, *hdc 2, (CC1) hdc 13, (MC) hdc 5, repeat from * 3 more times, join with sl st to ch 2 at beginning of rnd. [76 sts]

> ### Pro Tip
> Having trouble with your yarn tangling? Use a lazy Susan with pegs attached. Place your bobbins on the pegs, so that they travel with you as you crochet in the round!

**Rnd 6 (blo):** (MC) ch 2, turn, *hdc 4, (CC1) hdc 2, (MC) hdc 1, (CC1) hdc 1, (MC) hdc 6, (CC1) hdc 3, (MC) hdc 3, repeat from * 3 more times, join with sl st to ch 2 at beginning of rnd. [76 sts]

**Rnd 7 (flo):** (MC) ch 2, turn, *hdc 4, (CC1) hdc 2, (MC) hdc 6, (CC1) hdc 2, (MC) hdc 1, (CC1) hdc 2, (MC) hdc 3, repeat from * 3 more times, join with sl st to ch 2 at beginning of rnd. [76 sts]

**Rnd 8 (blo):** (MC) ch 2, turn, *hdc 2, (CC1) hdc 2,

(MC) hdc 1, (CC1) hdc 2, (MC) hdc 7, (CC1) hdc 1, (MC) hdc 5, repeat from * 3 more times, join with sl st to ch 2 at beginning of rnd. [76 sts]

Fasten off all bobbins, and we'll rejoin them when we reverse the arrows after the next rnd.

**Rnd 9 (flo):** (MC) ch 2, turn, hdc around, join with sl st to ch 2 at beginning of rnd. [76 sts]

**Rnd 10 (blo):** (MC) ch 2, turn, *hdc 5, (CC1) hdc 1, (MC) hdc 7, (CC1) hdc 2, (MC) hdc 1, (CC1) hdc 2, (MC) hdc 2, repeat from * 3 more times, to create the multicolored arrows alternate between CC1 and CC2 for each arrow, join with sl st to ch 2 at beginning of rnd. [76 sts]

**Rnd 11 (flo):** (MC) ch 2, turn, *hdc 3, (CC1) hdc 2, (MC) hdc 1, (CC1) hdc 2, (MC) hdc 6, (CC1) hdc 2, (MC) hdc 4, repeat from * 3 more times, join with sl st to ch 2 at beginning of rnd. [76 sts]

**Rnd 12 (blo):** (MC) ch 2, turn, *hdc 3, (CC1) hdc 3, (MC) hdc 6, (CC1) hdc 1, (MC) hdc 1, (CC1) hdc 2, (MC) hdc 4, repeat from * 3 more times, join with sl st to ch 2 at beginning of rnd. [76 sts]

**Rnd 13 (flo):** (MC) ch 2, turn, *hdc 5, (CC1) hdc 13, (MC) hdc 2, repeat from * 3 more times, join with sl st to ch 2 at beginning of rnd. [76 sts]

**Rnd 14 (blo):** (MC) ch 2, turn, *hdc 3, (CC1) hdc 3, (MC) hdc 6, (CC1) hdc 1, (MC) hdc 1, (CC1) hdc 2, (MC) hdc 4, repeat from * 3 more times, join with sl st to ch 2 at beginning of rnd. [76 sts]

**Rnd 15 (flo):** (MC) ch 2, turn, *hdc 3, (CC1) hdc 2,

(MC) hdc 1, (CC1) hdc 2, (MC) hdc 6, (CC1) hdc 2, (MC) hdc 4, repeat from * 3 more times, join with sl st to ch 2 at beginning of rnd. [76 sts]

**Rnd 16 (blo):** (MC) ch 2, turn, *hdc 5, (CC1) hdc 1, (MC) hdc 7, (CC1) hdc 2, (MC) hdc 1, (CC1) hdc 2, (MC) hdc 2, repeat from * 3 more times, join with sl st to ch 2 at beginning of rnd. [76 sts]

Fasten off all bobbins, except MC.

For the next 3 rnds: (MC) ch 2, turn, hdc around, join with sl st to ch 2 at beginning of rnd. [76 sts]

Fasten off, leaving a long tail for sewing the hat closed.

To close up the hat, thread long tail through a yarn needle, and sew a basting stitch (see page 21) around the top of the hat, then pull closed. Fasten off once hat is closed and weave in the ends.

## Attaching a Pom-Pom (Optional)

If you would like to add a faux fur pom-pom, as pictured in the sample, here is how you can do it. Position the pom-pom at the top of the hat, over the hole where you closed up the hat. Sew the pom-pom on top using an embroidery needle and thread, or if it has a snap closure position it on there and secure it. You can also make a pom-pom from yarn using a pom-pom maker and sew it in the same position.

*The Ombré Prism Wrap was inspired by light reflecting off glass crystals hanging from chandeliers in my parent's home. This design opens the door to a new way of using yarn with colorwork, which is using a multicolored skein of yarn to add more colors. With this pattern, you'll learn how to separate colors in a variegated skein of yarn, like Lion Brand Mandala Ombré, and how to use that with intarsia crochet. This pattern can be worn as a wrap with a blouse and jeans, or as a scarf to bundle up in the cold months. It has so many versatile ways to wear it that it will quickly become a wardrobe staple. Once you start doing colorwork this way, you won't want to stop!*

# Ombré Prism Wrap

## Pattern Level: Beginner

**Gauge:** 4" x 4" (10 x 10 cm) square = 14 hdc x 10 rows

**Wrap Dimensions:**
54" (137 cm) long x 13" (33 cm) wide

**Hook:** US J/10 6mm

**Yarn:**
- 2 skeins Lion Brand Jeans (Yarn Weight 4 Medium, 246 yds [225 m], 3.5 oz [100 g], 100 percent acrylic) in Denim (MC)
- 1 skein Lion Brand Mandala Ombré (Yarn Weight 4 Medium, 344 yds [315 m], 5.3 oz [150 g], 100 percent acrylic) in Mantra (CC)

**Approximate Yarn Yardage:**
MC = 400 yds (366 m)
CC = 100 yds (91 m)

**Abbreviations:**
ch = chain
hdc = half double crochet
st(s) = stitch(es)
MC = main color
CC = contrast color

## Chart

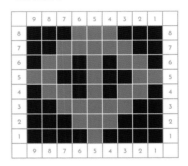

■ Main Color

■ Contrast Color

For chart notes and how to read a chart, see pages 15–17.

## Wrap

Before you begin the pattern, if you are using a variegated skein of yarn like Lion Brand Mandala Ombré, then you will want to start by deconstructing the skein to separate the different colors. Each time a new color starts, cut the yarn, and begin winding a new ball of yarn that can be used as a bobbin. My Lion Brand Mandala Ombré skein consisted of five different colors, so my diamonds on the wrap will be five different colors. However, since it is all the same yarn, it will be represented in the pattern as CC. You can use as many or as few colors as you'd like. It would even look great with just one color!

Once you have your yarn ready, start with the MC and ch 191.

The following row adds in CC. If you deconstructed a variegated skein for all of the colors, and want to get the effect that I have on mine, then you can add a new color of bobbin for the first five diamonds. Then reverse the colors for the other five. Carry the MC across the stitches when you are not using it.

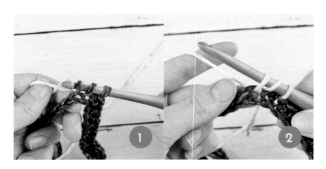

**Row 1:** (MC) starting in the third ch from the hook, *hdc 9, begin chart row 1 as follows, hdc 4, (CC) hdc 1 (you'll be joining a bobbin for this st while you hdc across the strand of ch sts), (see photos 1 and 2) (MC) hdc 4, end chart row 1, repeat from * 9 more times, hdc 9. [189 sts]

**Row 2:** (MC) ch 2 (ch 2 at the beginning of the row does not count as a st throughout the rest of the pattern), turn, *hdc 9, begin chart row 2 as follows, hdc 3, (CC) hdc 3, (MC) hdc 3, end chart row 2, repeat from * 9 more times, hdc 9. [189 sts]

**Row 3:** (MC) ch 2, turn, *hdc 9, begin chart row 3 as follows, hdc 2, (CC) hdc 5, (MC) hdc 2, end chart row 3, repeat from * 9 more times, hdc 9. [189 sts]

**Row 4:** (MC) ch 2, turn, *hdc 9, begin chart row 4 as follows, hdc 1, (CC) hdc 2, (MC) hdc 1, (CC) hdc 1, (MC) hdc 1, (CC) hdc 2, (MC) hdc 1, end chart row 4 as follows, repeat from * 9 more times, hdc 9. [189 sts]

**Row 5:** (CC) ch 2, turn, *hdc 9, begin chart row 5 as follows, hdc 2, (MC) hdc 2, (CC) hdc 1, (MC) hdc 2, (CC) hdc 2, end chart row 5, repeat from * 9 more times, hdc 9. [189 sts]

**Row 6:** (MC) ch 2, turn, *hdc 9, begin chart row 6 as follows, hdc 1, (CC) hdc 2, (MC) hdc 1, (CC) hdc 1, (MC) hdc 1, (CC) hdc 2, (MC) hdc 1, end chart row 6, repeat from * 9 more times, hdc 9. [189 sts]

**Row 7:** (MC) ch 2, turn, *hdc 9, begin chart row 7 as follows, hdc 2, (CC) hdc 5, (MC) hdc 2, end chart row 7, repeat from * 9 more times, hdc 9. [189 sts]

**Row 8:** (MC) ch 2, turn, *hdc 9, begin chart row 8 as follows, hdc 3, (CC) hdc 3, (MC) hdc 3, end chart row 8, repeat from * 9 more times, hdc 9. [189 sts]

Repeat rows 1 through 8 [189 sts] 3 more times for a total of 32 rows. When repeating row 1, you won't join a new bobbin each time, but continue using the ones you already have.

Fasten off and weave in the ends.

*The Mountaintop Cowl was inspired by the mountains that will always have a piece of my heart. For the majority of my life, I lived in a beach town along the California coast, but I was always drawn to the mountains just a few hours away. Now that I live close to them, I find myself adding mountains to my crochet designs all the time! With this pattern, you'll be able to continue practicing intarsia crochet in the round and really master that technique.*

# Mountaintop Cowl

## Pattern Level: Intermediate

**Gauge:** 4" x 4" (10 x 10 cm) square = 13 sc x 14 rows

**Dimensions:**
Height = 5.4" (13.5 cm)
Circumference = 32" (81 cm)

**Hook:** US J/10 6mm

**Yarn:** Lion Brand Re-Tweed (Yarn Weight 4 Medium, 202 yds [185 m], 3.5 oz [100 g], 40 percent wool, 40 percent polyester, 20 percent acrylic) in three colors:
- Dutch Blue (MC)
- Sleet (CC1)
- Hay (CC2)

**Approximate Yarn Yardage:**
MC = 150 yds (137 m)
CC1 = 75 yds (69 m)
CC2 = 50 yds (46 m)

**Abbreviations:**
ch = chain
st(s) = stitch(es)
sc = single crochet
rnd = round
blo = back loops only
flo = front loops only
sl st = slip stitch
MC = main color
CC1 = contrast color 1
CC2 = contrast color 2

# Mountaintop Cowl (Continued)

## Chart

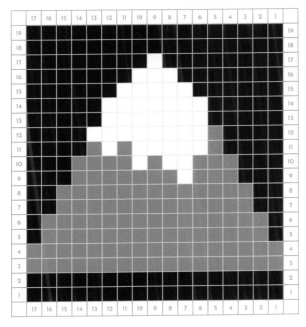

■ Main Color

▪ Contrast Color 1

□ Contrast Color 2

For chart notes and how to read a chart, see pages 15-17.

## Cowl

Starting with the MC, ch 105. Join the first and last chs together with a sl st. The first ch will no longer count as a st. [104 sts]

**Rnd 1:** ch 1 (ch 1 at the beginning of the rnd does not count as a st throughout the rest of the pattern), sc in each ch around, join with sl st to ch 1 at beginning of rnd. [104 sts]

**Rnd 2:** ch 1, turn, sc around, join with sl st to ch 1 at beginning of rnd. [104 sts]

For this next rnd, we'll be adding in a bobbin of CC1 each time we begin the chart pattern (see page 77 for details on this technique).

You'll begin using the chart on this page in the next rnd until you're done with the colorwork rounds.

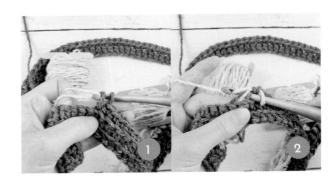

**Rnd 3:** (MC) ch 1, turn, *sc 9, begin using the chart, join a bobbin of (CC1) (see photo 1) then sc 17 carrying (MC) as you do each stitch (see photo 2). You should reach the end of the colorwork chart, if using. Repeat from * around, join with sl st to ch 1 at beginning of rnd. [104 sts]

# Mountaintop Cowl (Continued)

**Rnd 4:** (CC1) ch 1, turn, *begin using the chart, sc 17. You should reach the end of the colorwork chart, if using. (MC) sc 9, repeat from * around, join with sl st to ch 1 at beginning of rnd. [104 sts]

**Rnd 5:** (MC) ch 1, turn, *sc 9, begin using chart, sc 1, (CC1) sc 15, (MC) sc 1. You should reach the end of the colorwork chart, if using. Repeat from * around, join with sl st to ch 1 at beginning of rnd. [104 sts]

**Rnd 6:** (MC) ch 1, turn, *begin using chart, sc 1, (CC1) sc 15, (MC) sc 1. You should reach the end of the colorwork chart, if using. (MC) sc 9, repeat from * around, join with sl st to ch 1 at beginning of rnd. [104 sts]

**Rnd 7:** (MC) ch 1, turn *sc 9, begin using chart, sc 2, (CC1) sc 13, (MC) sc 2. You should reach the end of the colorwork chart, if using. Repeat from * around, join with sl st to ch 1 at beginning of rnd. [104 sts]

### Pro Tip

If you're seeing the MC peek through the contrast colored sts, pull the MC down slightly as you carry the color. This will have the yarn go toward the bottom of your stitches instead of the middle, where it can show.

**Rnd 8:** (MC) ch 1, turn, *begin using chart, sc 2, (CC1) sc 13, (MC) sc 2. You should reach the end of the colorwork chart, if using. (MC) sc 9, repeat from * around, join with sl st to ch 1 at beginning of rnd. [104 sts]

**Rnd 9:** (MC) ch 1, turn, *sc 9, begin using chart, sc 3, (CC1) sc 3, add (CC2) as a new bobbin then sc 1, (CC1) sc 7, (MC) sc 3. You should reach the end of the colorwork chart, if using. Repeat from * around, join with sl st to ch 1 at beginning of rnd. [104 sts]

**Rnd 10:** (MC) ch 1, turn, *begin using chart, sc 3, (CC1) sc 4, (CC2) sc 1, (CC1) sc 1, (CC2) sc 2, (CC1) sc 3, (MC) sc 3. You should reach the end of the colorwork chart, if using. (MC) sc 9, repeat from * around, join with sl st to ch 1 at beginning of rnd. [104 sts]

**Rnd 11:** (MC) ch 1, turn, *sc 9, begin using chart, sc 4, (CC1) sc 1, (CC2) sc 5, (CC1) sc 1, (CC2) sc 1, (CC1) sc 1, (MC) sc 4. You should reach the end of the colorwork chart, if using. Repeat from * around, join with sl st to ch 1 at beginning of rnd. [104 sts]

**Rnd 12:** (MC) ch 1, turn, *begin using chart, sc 4, (CC2) sc 8, (CC1) sc 1, (MC) sc 4. You should reach the end of the colorwork chart, if using. (MC) sc 9, repeat from * around, join with sl st to ch 1 at beginning of rnd. [104 sts]

Fasten off all CC1 bobbins. Continue using the MC and the CC2 bobbins.

**Rnd 13:** (MC) ch 1, turn, *sc 9, begin using chart, sc 5, (CC2) sc 7, (MC) sc 5. You should reach the end of the colorwork chart, if using. Repeat from * around, join with sl st to ch 1 at beginning of rnd. [104 sts]

**Rnd 14:** (MC) ch 1, turn, *begin using chart, sc 5, (CC2) sc 7, (MC) sc 5. You should reach the end of the colorwork chart, if using. (MC) sc 9, repeat from * around, join with sl st to ch 1 at beginning of rnd. [104 sts]

**Rnd 15:** (MC) ch 1, turn, *sc 9, begin using chart, sc 6, (CC2) sc 5, (MC) sc 6. You should reach the end of the colorwork chart, if using. Repeat from * around, join with sl st to ch 1 at beginning of rnd. [104 sts]

**Rnd 16:** (MC) ch 1, turn, *begin using chart, sc 7, (CC2) sc 3, (MC) sc 7. You should reach the end of the colorwork chart, if using. (MC) sc 9, repeat from * around, join with sl st to ch 1 at beginning of rnd. [104 sts]

**Rnd 17:** (MC) ch 1, turn, *sc 9, begin using chart, sc 8, (CC2) sc 1, (MC) sc 8. You should reach the end of the colorwork chart, if using. Repeat from * around, join with sl st to ch 1 at beginning of rnd. [104 sts]

Fasten off CC2, and continue using the MC.

**Rnds 18 and 19:** (MC) ch 1, turn, sc around, join with sl st to ch 1 at beginning of rnd. [104 sts]

Fasten off and weave in the ends.

*The Bloom Sweater was inspired by the colorful retro flower designs of the 1970s. With bold pops of color, this sweater design fully embraces the unique possibilities of intarsia crochet. The colorwork flower for this sweater will teach you how to do multicolored realistic designs with intarsia. By using multiple colors, you can create a beautiful realistic flower with yarn. Add the color block sleeves to it, and you have wearable art!*

# Bloom Sweater

## Pattern Level: Intermediate

**Gauge:** 4" x 4" (10 x 10 cm) square = 14 dc x 8 rows

**Sizes:** XS (S, M, L, XL, 2X, 3X, 4X, 5X)

**Finished Bust Measurements:**
- 33 (34 38, 43, 45, 50, 54, 57, 61)"
- 84 (86, 96.5, 109, 114, 127, 137, 145, 155) cm

**Finished Sweater Length:**
- 27 (27, 27, 28, 28, 28, 29, 29, 29)"
- 68.5 (68.5, 68.5, 71, 71, 71, 73.5, 73.5, 73.5) cm

**Finished Arm Length:**
- 16.5 (17, 17, 17.5, 18, 18, 18, 18.5, 18.5)"
- 42 (43, 43, 44.5, 45.5, 45.5, 45.5, 47, 47) cm

**Hook:** US H/8 5mm

**Yarn:** Lion Brand Basic Stitch Premium (Yarn Weight 4 Medium, 219 yds [220 m], 3.5 oz [100 g], 100 percent acrylic) in four colors:
- Saffron (MC)
- Ivy (CC1)
- Opal (CC2)
- Boysenberry (CC3)

**Approximate Yarn Yardage:**

MC = 648 (764, 901, 1038, 1144, 1287, 1480, 1659, 1715) yds (593 [699, 824, 950, 1046, 1176, 1353, 1516, 1568] m)

CC1 = 50 yds (46 m)

CC2 = 50 yds (46 m)

CC3 = 400 (400, 400, 450, 450, 450, 500, 500, 500) yds (336 [336, 336, 411, 411, 411, 457, 457, 457] m)

**Extra Materials:**

Yarn needle

**Abbreviations List:**

ch = chain

st(s) = stitch(es)

rnd(s) = round(s)

dc = double crochet

dec = decrease

sl st = slip stitch

fpdc = front post double crochet

bpdc = back post double crochet

MC = main color

CC1 = contrast color 1

CC2 = contrast color 2

CC3 = contrast color 3

## Chart

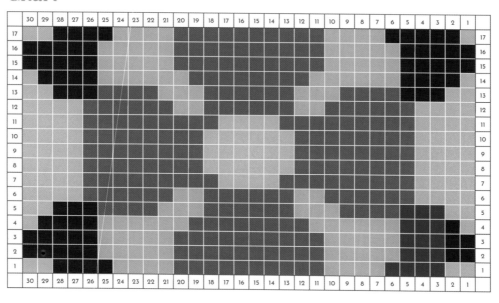

 Main Color

■ Contrast Color 1

■ Contrast Color 2

■ Contrast Color 3

For chart notes and how to read a chart, see pages 15–17.

## Front Panel (Make 1)

Starting with MC, ch 58 (62, 70, 78, 82, 90, 98, 102, 110).

**Row 1:** starting in third ch from hook, dc 56 (60, 68, 76, 80, 88, 96, 100, 108). [56 (60, 68, 76, 80, 88, 96, 100, 108) sts]

**Row 2:** ch 2 (ch 2 at the beginning of the row does not count as a st throughout the rest of the pattern), turn, *dc 2, fpdc 2, repeat from * across. [56 (60, 68, 76, 80, 88, 96, 100, 108) sts]

**Row 3:** ch 2, turn, *bpdc 2, dc 2, repeat from * across. [56 (60, 68, 76, 80, 88, 96, 100, 108) sts]

**Rows 4 through 9:** repeat rows 2 and 3

For next 14 (14, 14, 15, 15, 15, 16, 16, 16) rows: ch 2, turn, dc across. [56 (60, 68, 76, 80, 88, 96, 100, 108) sts]

Starting with this next row, we will be doing the colorwork flower. Since we are using intarsia crochet, we will join new bobbins at each of the color changes. If you would like to have fewer bobbins, you can carry the same color to the next section of that color when they are close together.

**Chart Row 1:** starting with MC, ch 2, turn, dc 13 (15, 19, 23, 25, 29, 33, 35, 39), place stitch marker in last st you did to mark the last st before the colorwork starts. Crochet row 1 of the chart, which would read: (MC) dc 2, (CC1) dc 4, (CC2) dc 4, (CC3) dc 10, (CC2) dc 4, (CC1) dc 4, (MC) dc 2. After completing the chart, dc 1 and place marker in this st, dc to end. [56 (60, 68, 76, 80, 88, 96, 100, 108) sts] You should have one st marker on each side of the charted stitches.

For the next 16 rows: starting with MC, ch 2, dc to stitch marker including the stitch it is in, crochet next row of the colorwork, and then dc to end with MC.

For next 14 (14, 14, 15, 15, 15, 16, 16, 16) rows: ch 2, turn, dc across. [56 (60, 68, 76, 80, 88, 96, 100, 108) sts]

You should end with 54 (54, 54, 56, 56, 56, 58, 58, 58) rows, which will be approximately 27 (27, 27, 28, 28, 28, 29, 29, 29)" or 68.5 (68.5, 68.5, 71, 71, 71, 73.5, 73.5, 73.5) cm long.

Fasten off.

## Back Panel (Make 1)

Using the MC, ch 58 (62, 70, 78, 82, 90, 98, 102, 110).

**Row 1:** starting in third ch from hook, dc 56 (60, 68, 76, 80, 88, 96, 100, 108). [56 (60, 68, 76, 80, 88, 96, 100, 108) sts]

**Row 2:** ch 2, turn, *dc 2, fpdc 2, repeat from * across. [56 (60, 68, 76, 80, 88, 96, 100, 108)]

**Row 3:** ch 2, turn, *bpdc 2, dc 2, repeat from * across. [56 (60, 68, 76, 80, 88, 96, 100, 108)]

**Rows 4 through 9:** repeat rows 2 and 3.

**Row 10:** ch 2, turn, dc across. [56 (60, 68, 76, 80, 88, 96, 100, 108)]

Repeat row 10 until you have 54 (54, 54, 56, 56, 56, 58, 58, 58) rows total. Fasten off and weave in the ends.

## Seaming

Once both panels are done, you'll seam both pieces together. See pages 18-21 for different seaming methods.

On the left and right sides, measure down approximately 6 (7, 7, 8, 8, 9, 9, 10, 10)" or 15 (18, 18, 20, 20, 23, 23, 25.5, 25.5) cm from the top. Mark that point, and you will work up to this point when seaming the sides. This helps form the armhole.

# Bloom Sweater (Continued)

## Sleeves (Make Two, One on Each Armhole)

Using the CC3, use a sl st to join the yarn to the top of one of the side seams in the underarm of the sweater.

**Rnd 1:** ch 2, dc 44 (48, 52, 56, 60, 64, 68, 72, 76) around the armhole, join with sl st to ch 2 at beginning of rnd. [44 (48, 52, 56, 60, 64, 68, 72, 76) sts]

**Rnd 2:** ch 2, turn, dc around, join with sl st to ch 2 at beg of rnd. [44 (48, 52, 56, 60, 64, 68, 72, 76) sts]

Repeat rnd 2 till your sleeve reaches the length to the elbow. Approx. 8 (9, 9, 9, 10, 10, 10, 11, 11)" or 20 (23, 23, 23, 25.5, 25.5, 25.5, 28, 28) cm in length.

**Next Rnd:** ch 2, turn, *dc 9 (10, 11, 12, 13, 14, 15, 16, 17), dc dec 1, repeat from * around, join with sl st to ch 2 at beginning of rnd. [40 (44, 48, 52, 56, 60, 64, 68, 72) sts]

**Next Rnd:** ch 2, turn, dc around, join with sl st to ch 2 at beg of rnd. [40 (44, 48, 52, 56, 60, 64, 68, 72) sts]

**Next Rnd:** ch 2, turn, *dc 8 (9, 10, 11, 12, 13, 14, 15, 16), dc dec 1, repeat from * around, join with sl st to ch 2 at beginning of rnd. [36 (40, 44, 48, 52, 56, 60, 64, 68) sts]

**Next Rnd:** ch 2, turn, dc around, join with sl st to ch 2 at beginning of rnd. [36 (40, 44, 48, 52, 56, 60, 64, 68) sts]

Repeat last rnd till you've crocheted to 3" (7.5 cm) above the wrist. Approx. 7 (8, 8, 8, 9, 9, 9, 10, 10)" or 18 (20, 20, 20, 23, 23, 23, 25.5 25.5) cm in length.

**Next rnd:** ch 2, turn, *dc 7 (8, 9, 10, 11, 12, 13, 14, 15), dc dec 1, repeat from * around, join with sl st to ch 2 at beginning of rnd. [32 (36, 40, 44, 48, 52, 56, 60, 64) sts]

**Next rnd:** ch 2, turn, dc around, join with sl st to ch 2 at beginning of rnd.

**Next rnd:** ch 2, turn, *dc 6 (7, 8, 9, 10, 11, 12, 13, 14), dc dec 1, repeat from * around, join with sl st to ch 2 at beginning of rnd. [28 (32, 36, 40, 44, 48, 52, 56, 60) sts]

**Next rnd:** ch 2, turn, dc around, join with sl st to ch 2 at beginning of rnd.

If you would like the armhole to be decreased by more, continue repeating the decrease rnd with one less dc before the dc dec. You want to make sure that each rnd ends with a stitch count that is divisible by 4.

**Next six rnds:** ch 2, *dc 2, fpdc 2, repeat from * around. [28, 32, 36, 40, 44, 48, 52, 56, 60) sts]

Your sleeves should have approximately 33 (34, 34, 35, 36, 36, 36, 37, 37) rnds.

Fasten off and weave in ends. Repeat for opposite sleeve.

*The Trailhead Ruana was inspired by long hikes exploring trails through the wilderness, and all of the beautiful pieces of nature you can see. It showcases acorns, pine cones and arrows to help point you in the right direction on your adventures. I love cozy garments that can be worn in multiple ways, and that's why ruanas are one of my favorite garments to make. You can think of a ruana as a combination of a poncho, a wrap and a cardigan all in one. It's an oversized rectangle that has a front split down the middle like a cardigan and open sides in the style of a poncho. Garment design will give you lots of practice in combining multiple techniques; specifically intarsia and tapestry crochet. By combining bobbins and carrying yarn, you'll be able to still have a clean look to your project without juggling a million bobbins.*

# Trailhead Ruana

## Pattern Level: Intermediate

**Gauge:** 4" x 4" (10 x 10 cm) square = 14 hdc x 9 rows

**Sizes:** One size

This pattern is one size fits all, but there are a few things you can do to customize it for the best fit. You can adjust the width by adding rows before doing the colorwork. Add approximately two rows for every inch you'd like to add. I recommend doing the same amount of added rows at both the beginning and end of the ruana, so that it is even on both sides. If you'd like to adjust the length, add three or four stitches for every inch you'd like to add. I recommend putting them at the beginning and end of each row in order for them to be even, then add those stitch amounts to the stitches done before the colorwork on each row.

**Finished Dimensions:**
- 34" (86 cm) wide x 67" (170 cm) long

**Hook:** US J/10 6mm

**Yarn:** Lion Brand Heartland (Yarn Weight 4 Medium, 251 yds [230 m], 5 oz [142 g], 100 percent acrylic) in five colors:

- Mammoth Cave (MC)
- Olympic (CC1)
- Kings Canyon (CC2)
- Yosemite (CC3)
- Yellowstone (CC4)

**Approximate Yarn Yardage:**
MC = 753 yds (689 m)
CC1 = 150 yds (137 m)
CC2 = 502 yds (460 m)
CC3 = 150 yds (137 m)
CC4 = 150 yds (137 m)

**Abbreviations:**
ch(s) = chain(s)
hdc = half double crochet
st(s) = stitch(es)
MC = main color
CC1 = contrast color 1
CC2 = contrast color 2
CC3 = contrast color 3
CC4 = contrast color 4

## Charts

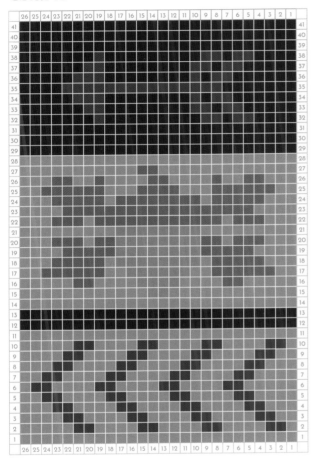 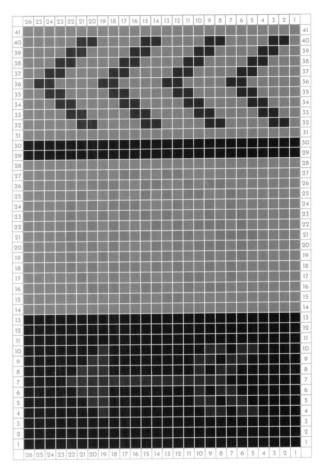

■ Main Color

■ Contrast Color 1

■ Contrast Color 2

■ Contrast Color 3

■ Contrast Color 4

For chart notes and how to read a chart, see pages 15–17.

## Ruana

Starting with MC, ch 235.

**Row 1:** starting in third ch from hook, hdc 233. [233 sts]

**Row 2:** ch 2 (ch 2 at the beginning of the row does not count as a st throughout the rest of the pattern), turn, hdc across. [233 sts]

You'll now begin using bobbins to do the colorwork for this section. We'll be doing a combination of intarsia crochet and tapestry crochet with this pattern. You'll join a bobbin at each point where the colorwork begins, and then carry the unused color amidst that section until it ends. There are 6 total sections, so you'll need 6 bobbins in CC1 to start, and then 6 bobbins of each color for the other colors that are a part of the main colorwork sections.

**Row 3:** (MC) ch 2, turn, *hdc 12, join bobbin of CC1 then (CC1) hdc 2, (MC) hdc 4, (CC1) hdc 2, (MC) hdc 4, (CC1) hdc 2, (MC) hdc 4, (CC1) hdc 2, (MC) hdc 5, repeat from * 5 more times, hdc 11. [233 sts]

**Row 4:** (MC) ch 2, turn, *hdc 15, (CC1) hdc 2, (MC) hdc 4, (CC1) hdc 2, (MC) hdc 4, (CC1) hdc 2, (MC) hdc 4, (CC1) hdc 2, (MC) hdc 2, repeat from * 5 more times, hdc 11. [233 sts]

**Row 5:** (MC) ch 2, turn, *hdc 14, (CC1) hdc 2, (MC) hdc 4, (CC1) hdc 2, (MC) hdc 4, (CC1) hdc 2, (MC) hdc 4, (CC1) hdc 2, (MC) hdc 3, repeat from * 5 more times, hdc 11. [233 sts]

**Row 6:** (MC) ch 2, turn, *hdc 13, (CC1) hdc 2, (MC) hdc 4, (CC1) hdc 2, (MC) hdc 4, (CC1) hdc 2, (MC) hdc 4, (CC1) hdc 2, (MC) hdc 4, repeat from * 5 more times, hdc 11. [233 sts]

**Row 7:** (MC) ch 2, turn, *hdc 16, (CC1) hdc 2, (MC) hdc 4, (CC1) hdc 2, (MC) hdc 4, (CC1) hdc 2, (MC) hdc 4, (CC1) hdc 2, (MC) hdc 1, repeat from * 5 more times, hdc 11. [233 sts]

**Row 8:** (MC) ch 2, turn, *hdc 13, (CC1) hdc 2, (MC) hdc 4, (CC1) hdc 2, (MC) hdc 4, (CC1) hdc 2, (MC) hdc 4, (CC1) hdc 2, (MC) hdc 4, repeat from * 5 more times, hdc 11. [233 sts]

**Row 9:** (MC) ch 2, turn, *hdc 14, (CC1) hdc 2, (MC) hdc 4, (CC1) hdc 2, (MC) hdc 4, (CC1) hdc 2, (MC) hdc 4, (CC1) hdc 2, (MC) hdc 3, repeat from * 5 more times, hdc 11. [233 sts]

**Row 10:** (MC) ch 2, turn, *hdc 15, (CC1) hdc 2, (MC) hdc 4, (CC1) hdc 2, (MC) hdc 4, (CC1) hdc 2, (MC) hdc 4, (CC1) hdc 2, (MC) hdc 2, repeat from * 5 more times, hdc 11. [233 sts]

**Row 11:** (MC) ch 2, turn, *hdc 12, (CC1) hdc 2, (MC) hdc 4, (CC1) hdc 2, (MC) hdc 4, (CC1) hdc 2, (MC) hdc 4, (CC1) hdc 2, (MC) hdc 5, repeat from * 5 more times, hdc 11. [233 sts]

Fasten off CC1. You'll rejoin CC1 later on to repeat rows 3 through 11. Continue using the MC to do the next row.

**Row 12:** (MC) ch 2, turn, hdc across. [233 sts]

You'll now join CC2 for two rows to create a stripe. Use the technique used for the Desert Diamonds Top in Chapter 1 to carry the MC up these next two rows to use on row 15.

**Rows 13 and 14:** (CC2) ch 2, turn, hdc across. [233 sts]

**Row 15:** (MC) ch 2, turn, hdc across. [233 sts]

**Row 16:** (MC) ch 2, turn, *hdc 23, join bobbin of CC3 then, (CC3) hdc 2, (MC) hdc 12, repeat from * 5 more times, hdc 11. [233 sts]

**Row 17:** (MC) ch 2, turn, *hdc 16, join bobbin of CC4 then (CC4) hdc 2, (MC) hdc 4, (CC3) hdc 4, (MC) hdc 4, (CC4) hdc 2, (MC) hdc 5, repeat from * 5 more times, hdc 11. [233 sts]

**Row 18:** (MC) ch 2, turn, *hdc 13, (CC4) hdc 6, (MC) hdc 2, (CC3) hdc 6, (MC) hdc 2, (CC4) hdc 6, (MC) hdc 2, repeat from * 5 more times, hdc 11. [233 sts]

**Row 19:** (MC) ch 2, turn, *hdc 14, (CC4) hdc 5, (MC) hdc 1, (CC3) hdc 8, (MC) hdc 1, (CC4) hdc 5, (MC) hdc 3, repeat from * 5 more times, hdc 11. [233 sts]

**Row 20:** (MC) ch 2, turn, *hdc 15, (CC4) hdc 5, (CC3) hdc 8, (CC4) hdc 5, (MC) hdc 4, repeat from * 5 more times, hdc 11. [233 sts]

**Row 21:** (MC) ch 2, turn, *hdc 14, (CC4) hdc 3, (MC) hdc 1, (CC4) hdc 2, (CC3) hdc 8, (CC4) hdc 2, (MC) hdc 1, (CC4) hdc 3, (MC) hdc 3, repeat from * 5 more times, hdc 11. [233 sts]

**Row 22:** (MC) ch 2, turn, *hdc 20, (CC3) hdc 8, (MC) hdc 9, repeat from * 5 more times, hdc 11. [233 sts]

Fasten off CC3, and continue with MC and CC4 for the following rows.

**Row 23:** (MC) ch 2, turn, *hdc 14, (CC4) hdc 3, (MC) hdc 1, (CC4) hdc 12, (MC) hdc 1, (CC4) hdc 3, (MC) hdc 3, repeat from * 5 more times, hdc 11. [233 sts]

**Row 24:** (MC) ch 2, turn, *hdc 15, (CC4) hdc 18, (MC) hdc 4, repeat from * 5 more times, hdc 11. [233 sts]

**Row 25:** (MC) ch 2, turn, *hdc 14, (CC4) hdc 5, (MC) hdc 1, (CC4) hdc 8, (MC) hdc 1, (CC4) hdc 5, (MC) hdc 3, repeat from * 5 more times, hdc 11. [233 sts]

**Row 26:** (MC) ch 2, turn, *hdc 13, (CC4) hdc 6, (MC) hdc 3, (CC4) hdc 4, (MC) hdc 3, (CC4) hdc 6, (MC) hdc 2, repeat from * 5 more times, hdc 11. [233 sts]

**Row 27:** (MC) ch 2, turn, *hdc 14, (CC4) hdc 2, (MC) hdc 2, (CC4) hdc 1, (MC) hdc 4, (CC4) hdc 2, (MC) hdc 4, (CC4) hdc 1, (MC) hdc 2, (CC4) hdc 2, (MC) hdc 3, repeat from * 5 more times, hdc 11. [233 sts]

**Row 28:** (MC) ch 2, turn, *hdc 22, (CC4) hdc 2, (MC) hdc 13, repeat from * 5 more times, hdc 11. [233 sts]

Fasten off CC4, and continue with the MC.

**Row 29:** (MC) ch 2, turn, hdc across. [233 sts]

Fasten off MC, and join CC2 to use for the following rnds till the MC is used again.

**Rows 30 through 32:** (CC2) ch 2, turn, hdc across. [233 sts]

**Row 33:** (CC2) ch 2, turn, *hdc 15, (CC1) hdc 2, (CC2) hdc 1, (CC1) hdc 2, (CC2) hdc 9, (CC1) hdc 1, (CC2) hdc 7, repeat from * 5 more times, hdc 11. [233 sts]

**Row 34:** (CC2) ch 2, turn, *hdc 17, (CC1) hdc 2, (CC2) hdc 8, (CC1) hdc 2, (CC2) hdc 1, (CC1) hdc 2, (CC2) hdc 5, repeat from * 5 more times, hdc 11. [233 sts]

**Row 35:** (CC2) ch 2, turn, *hdc 18, (CC1) hdc 2, (CC2) hdc 1, (CC1) hdc 1, (CC2) hdc 8, (CC1) hdc 3, (CC2) hdc 5, repeat from * 5 more times, hdc 5. [233 sts]

**Row 36:** (CC2) ch 2, turn, *hdc 15, (CC1) hdc 15, (CC2) hdc 7, repeat from * 5 more times, hdc 11. [233 sts]

**Row 37:** (CC2) ch 2, turn, *hdc 17, (CC1) hdc 2, (CC2) hdc 1, (CC1) hdc 1, (CC2) hdc 8, (CC1) hdc 3, (CC2) hdc 5, repeat from * 5 more times, hdc 11. [233 sts]

**Row 38:** (CC2) ch 2, turn, *hdc 17, (CC1) hdc 2, (CC2) hdc 8, (CC1) hdc 2, (CC2) hdc 1, (CC1) hdc 2, (CC2) hdc 5, repeat from * 5 more times, hdc 11. [233 sts]

**Row 39:** (CC2) ch 2, turn, *hdc 15, (CC1) hdc 2, (CC2) hdc 1, (CC1) hdc 2, (CC2) hdc 9, (CC1) hdc 1, (CC2) hdc 7, repeat from * 5 more times, hdc 11. [233 sts]

Fasten off CC1, and continue using CC2.

**Row 40:** (CC2) ch 2, turn, hdc across. [233 sts]

We'll now be working off of this panel to create the second side of the ruana. The next three rows do not go all the way down along the panel, but go just below halfway to start the shaping for when we split.

**Rows 41 and 42:** (CC2) ch 2, turn, hdc 107. [107 sts]

**Row 43:** (CC2) ch 2, turn, hdc 107, ch 128. [233 sts]

**Row 44:** (CC2) turn, starting in third ch from hook, hdc across (the skipped chs at the beginning of the row do not count as a stitch). [233 sts]

We've now created a new panel that is worked off of the other one. You'll continue the rest of the pattern off of the one you just made.

**Rows 45 through 52:** repeat rows 31 through 38. [233 sts]

**Row 53:** (CC2) ch 2, turn, hdc across. [233 sts]

Fasten off CC2 and the other colors used for the arrows. Rejoin MC, and you'll now use CC3 again.

**Row 54:** (MC) ch 2, turn, *hdc 21, (CC3) hdc 2, (MC) hdc 2, (CC3) hdc 2, (MC) hdc 10, repeat from * 5 more times, hdc 11. [233 sts]

**Row 55:** (MC) ch 2, turn, *hdc 17, (CC3) hdc 2, (MC) hdc 1, (CC3) hdc 1, (MC) hdc 2, (CC3) hdc 2, (MC) hdc 2, (CC3) hdc 3, (MC) hdc 7, repeat from * 5 more times, hdc 11. [233 sts]

**Row 56:** (MC) ch 2, turn, *hdc 17, (CC3) hdc 1, (MC) hdc 2, (CC3) hdc 1, (MC) hdc 2, (CC3) hdc 1, (MC) hdc 1, (CC3) hdc 1, (MC) hdc 1, (CC3) hdc 2, (MC) hdc 2, (CC3) hdc 1, (MC) hdc 5, repeat from * 5 more times, hdc 11. [233 sts]

**Row 57:** (MC) ch 2, turn, *hdc 16, (CC3) hdc 1, (MC) hdc 1, (CC3) hdc 1, (MC) hdc 2, (CC3) hdc 1, (MC) hdc 3, (CC3) hdc 3, (MC) hdc 1, (CC3) hdc 1, (MC) hdc 1, (CC3) hdc 1, (MC) hdc 5, repeat from * 5 more times, hdc 11. [233 sts]

**Row 58:** (MC) ch 2, turn, *hdc 16, (CC3) hdc 1, (MC) hdc 2, (CC3) hdc 1, (MC) hdc 1, (CC3) hdc 1, (MC) hdc 1, (CC3) hdc 1, (MC) hdc 1, (CC3) hdc 1, (MC) hdc 3, (CC3) hdc 1, (MC) hdc 1, (CC3) hdc 2, (MC) hdc 4, repeat from * 5 more times, hdc 11. [233 sts]

**Row 59:** (MC) ch 2, turn, *hdc 15, (CC3) hdc 1, (MC) hdc 1, (CC3) hdc 3, (MC) hdc 1, (CC3) hdc 1, (MC) hdc 1, (CC3) hdc 1, (MC) hdc 3, (CC3) hdc 1, (MC) hdc 1, (CC3) hdc 1, (MC) hdc 1, (CC3) hdc 1, (MC) hdc 5, repeat from * 5 more times, hdc 11. [233 sts]

**Row 60:** (MC) ch 2, turn, *hdc 16, (CC3) hdc 2, (MC) hdc 2, (CC3) hdc 2, (MC) hdc 1, (CC3) hdc 1, (MC) hdc 2, (CC3) hdc 2, (MC) hdc 2, (CC3) hdc 4, (MC) hdc 3, repeat from * 5 more times, hdc 11. [233 sts]

**Row 61:** (MC) ch 2, turn, *hdc 15, (CC3) hdc 1, (MC) hdc 1, (CC3) hdc 3, (MC) hdc 1, (CC3) hdc 1, (MC) hdc 1, (CC3) hdc 1, (MC) hdc 3, (CC3) hdc 1, (MC) hdc 1, (CC3) hdc 1, (MC) hdc 1, (CC3) hdc 1, (MC) hdc 5, repeat from * 5 more times, hdc 11. [233 sts]

**Row 62:** (MC) ch 2, turn, *hdc 16, (CC3) hdc 1, (MC) hdc 2, (CC3) hdc 1, (MC) hdc 1, (CC3) hdc 1, (MC) hdc 1, (CC3) hdc 1, (MC) hdc 1, (CC3) hdc 1, (MC) hdc 3, (CC3) hdc 1, (MC) hdc 1, (CC3) hdc 2, (MC) hdc 4, repeat from * 5 more times, hdc 11. [233 sts]

**Row 63:** (MC) ch 2, turn, *hdc 16, (CC3) hdc 1, (MC) hdc 1, (CC3) hdc 1, (MC) hdc 2, (CC3) hdc 1, (MC) hdc 3, (CC3) hdc 3, (MC) hdc 1, (CC3) hdc 1, (MC) hdc 1, (CC3) hdc 1, (MC) hdc 5, repeat from * 5 more times, hdc 11. [233 sts]

**Row 64:** (MC) ch 2, turn, *hdc 17, (CC3) hdc 1, (MC) hdc 2, (CC3) hdc 1, (MC) hdc 2, (CC3) hdc 1, (MC) hdc 1, (CC3) hdc 1, (MC) hdc 1, (CC3) hdc 2, (MC) hdc 2, (CC3) hdc 1, (MC) hdc 5, repeat from * 5 more times, hdc 11. [233 sts]

**Row 65:** (MC) ch 2, turn, *hdc 17, (CC3) hdc 2, (MC) hdc 1, (CC3) hdc 1, (MC) hdc 2, (CC3) hdc 2, (MC) hdc 2, (CC3) hdc 3, (MC) hdc 7, repeat from * 5 more times, hdc 11. [233 sts]

**Row 66:** (MC) ch 2, turn, *hdc 21, (CC3) hdc 2, (MC) hdc 2, (CC3) hdc 2, (MC) hdc 10, repeat from * 5 more times, hdc 11. [233 sts]

Fasten off CC3, and continue with MC and CC1 for the following rows.

**Rows 67 through 78:** repeat rows 3 through 11.

Fasten off CC1 and continue with MC.

**Rows 79 and 80:** (MC) ch 2, turn, hdc across. [233 sts]

Fasten off and weave in all the ends.

# Fair Isle Crochet

**Get ready for the wonderful world of fair isle crochet!** This is the crochet version of stranded knitting that is used to create gorgeous colorwork designs. Fair isle crochet centers around detailed designs featuring small and large motifs combined to re-create the style of Fair Isle knitting. It also changes the way colors are carried by using floats and is most often done using the waistcoat stitch.

Often fair isle crochet is mistakenly defined as being any crochet project done with the waistcoat stitch. However, when studying the history of fair isle knitting, I learned that it stems from the way the colors are carried. Knitters from Fair Isle created a technique in which they carry the yarn by using floats, which are small strands of yarn stretched between stitches. They also use a distinct style of densely patterned yoke sweaters and accessories that feature designs such as snowflakes, stars, trees and other geometric shapes. They can range from having two colors or ten! As long as you use just two colors per row, you can create beautiful multicolored designs with this technique.

I find fair isle crochet to be the technique that lends itself best to creating projects that look just like stranded knitting, since it is based around the same technique. While crocheting the designs, you use floats that stretch along the back of your work between stitches, instead of carrying the yarn through every stitch. Though you can use any stitch to do fair isle crochet, my favorite stitch to use is the waistcoat stitch. The waistcoat stitch creates a knit-like stitch that stacks colorwork stitches on each other more easily, which in turn creates cleaner looking colorwork. If you love the look of knit sweaters, then you're going to love how you'll be able to tell people that your fair isle crochet project is crochet instead of a knit!

In this chapter, I'll be walking you through each technique you'll need to do fair isle crochet. I'll cover how to create floats on the back of your work, maintaining good tension with your floats and how to do the waistcoat stitch. You're going to love the projects in this chapter! From the cozy Winter's Breath Scarf (page 119) to the knit-looking Forest Walk Sweater (page 146), you'll have so much fun learning this technique with these projects.

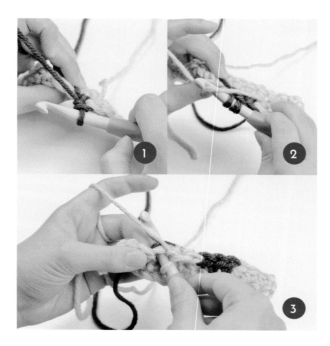

## Basic Fair Isle Techniques

### How to Carry Yarn Using Floats

Floats are the distinct feature that sets fair isle crochet apart from the other colorwork techniques. Just like the others each have their own way to carry or use colors, this one uses floats. Floats are small strands of yarn that stretch across multiple stitches to the next point where you need the color. This could range from one to ten or more stitches. Follow the steps below to start doing fair isle crochet using floats.

**Step 1** (photo 1): As you are crocheting, when you stop using one color to start with another one, you'll drop that previous color and pick up the new one.

**Step 2** (photo 2): Do the amount of stitches you need with the new color, and when you switch back to the previous one, you'll stretch the yarn from the point where you left it. This will make a small strand of yarn stretch behind the stitches.

**Step 3** (photo 3): If your colorwork is spaced farther than three or four stitches, then you will want to lock your floats to your work. To do that, every three or four stitches, crochet around the yarn you're carrying as if you're doing tapestry crochet for one stitch. This helps prevent your floats from being too large in the back. It also helps with the overall tension of your project.

### Using the Waistcoat (or Knit) Stitch

When doing fair isle crochet, one of the most common stitches used is the waistcoat stitch. It mimics the look of knitted stitches, making your crochet project look like it is a knit. It also works very well with using floats to carry your yarn, since you don't have to carry through each of the stitches. The stitch itself is a modification of the single crochet stitch, worked in the V of the stitch instead of through the stitch loops. To do the stitch:

**Step 1** (photo 1 on opposite page): Crochet at least one row of single crochet, which will be the foundation row for the waistcoat stitch. On the following row, you'll begin the waistcoat stitch.

**Step 2** (photo 2 on opposite page): To do the first waistcoat stitch, locate the V of the stitch you will be working through.

**Step 3** (photo 3 on opposite page): Insert your hook through the V of the stitch.

**Step 4** (photo 4 on opposite page): Yarn over and finish your stitch like a normal single crochet stitch.

**Step 5:** Repeat steps 3 and 4 until you are done with the row.

**Step 6** (photo 5 on opposite page): On the next row, you'll work your single crochet stitches through the Vs of the stitches that you did in the previous row. Since you've already done one row, they will be more apparent this time.

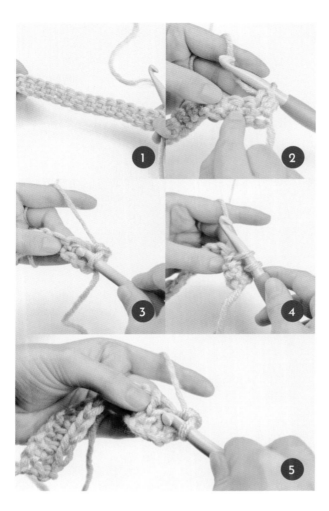

**Step 7:** While doing the waistcoat stitch, keep in mind that it will look different when doing it worked flat versus in the round. The stitches will stack easier when worked in the round and will be done the same way for the whole project. The Vs will always lie in the same direction. When doing it flat, the Vs will be upside-down.

## How to Do Fair Isle Crochet Worked Flat and in the Round:

Like the other colorwork techniques, fair isle is done slightly differently when it's worked flat versus in the round. My favorite way to use it is in the round, but doing it flat works as well! Here are some tips on how to do both ways:

### Worked Flat

- **Carrying Yarn:** When doing fair isle crochet worked flat, you will carry the yarn using floats, which will lock the floats on the back of your work. When working on the right side, your floats will be along the wrong side of the work, which is the side that is facing away from you. If there are a lot of stitches in between portions of colorwork., lock the yarn for one stitch by carrying it every three to four stitches. When working on the wrong side, it faces you and your floats will be along that side.

- **Using the Waistcoat Stitch:** When using the waistcoat stitch worked flat, it will look different than when done in the round. It will be done like normal on the right side. However, on the wrong side, the Vs of the stitches are upside-down, so you will want to make sure you go through the upside-down Vs to help your stitches stack easier.

### Worked in the Round

- **Carrying Yarn:** When doing fair isle in the round, typically you always work on the right side. You will always carry your yarn on the inside of your project, which is the wrong side. Use the same technique to lock your floats in place as you do when worked flat.

- **Using the Waistcoat Stitch:** When you do the waistcoat stitch in the round, you will want to stay working on the right side the entire time. The stitches will always stack on each other since the Vs are always right-side up. It will help the slanting of the stitches to be hardly noticeable.

*The Falling Snowflakes Hat was inspired by one of my favorite motifs in fair isle knitting— the snowflake. I love the simplicity of this style of snowflake and how it looks beautiful on any project. With this design, you'll learn how to do fair isle crochet in the round. We'll start first by using the normal single crochet in the back-loops-only technique we've been using. This way you can get comfortable using floats to carry your yarn without needing to learn a new stitch. I think you're going to love this one!*

# Falling Snowflakes Hat

## Pattern Level: Beginner

**Gauge:** 4″ x 4″ (10 x 10 cm) square = 11 sc x 12 rows

**Gauge for Brim:** 4″ x 4″ (10 x 10 cm) square (worked in alternating rows of blo and flo) = 11 dc x 5 rows

**Hook:** US L/11 8mm

**Hat Measurements:**
- Circumference: 21″ (53 cm)
- Height: 8″ (20 cm)

**Yarn:** Lion Brand Color Made Easy (Yarn Weight 5 Bulky, 247 yds [226 m], 7 oz [200 g], 100 percent acrylic) in two colors:
- Pomegranate (MC)
- Alabaster (CC)

**Approximate Yarn Yardage:**
MC = 100 yds (92 m)
CC = 50 yds (46 m)

**Extra Materials:**
Yarn needle

**Abbreviations:**
ch = chain
st(s) = stitch(es)
sc = single crochet
dc = double crochet
rnd = round
sl st = slip stitch
blo = back loops only
flo = front loops only
sl st = slip stitch
MC = main color
CC = contrast color

# Falling Snowflakes Hat (Continued)

## Chart

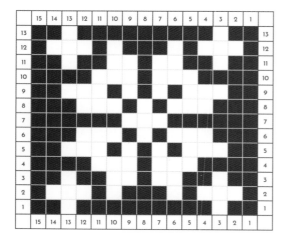

■ Main Color

□ Contrast Color

For chart notes and how to read a chart, see pages 15-17.

## Brim

Starting with MC, ch 8.

**Row 1:** starting in third ch from hook, dc 6. [6 sts]

**Row 2:** ch 2 (ch 2 at the beginning of the row does not count as a st throughout the rest of the pattern), turn, dc across in the blo. [6 sts]

**Row 3:** ch 2, turn, dc across in the flo. [6 sts]

For the next 24 rows, alternate between repeating rows 2 and 3.

Once you're done with those rows, join the two ends of your brim right sides together with a sl st. Turn it right-side out, and then you'll move on to the body of the hat.

## Body of Hat

**Foundation Rnd:** (MC) ch 1, sc around the top of the brim of the hat (working approximately two sts at the end of each row of the brim, adding an extra stitch every fourth row) for a total of 60 sts, join with sl st to ch 1 at beginning of rnd. [60 sts]

You'll now work the rest of the hat through the blo. This helps offset the slanting that occurs when doing colorwork in the rnd. The following rnds correspond with the same row number on the chart, beginning with rnd 1 and row 1.

**Rnd 1:** (MC) ch 1 (ch 1 at the beginning of the rnd does not count as a st throughout the rest of the pattern), *sc 2, (CC) sc 1, (MC) sc 9, (CC) sc 1, (MC) sc 2, repeat from * around, join with sl st to ch 1 at beginning of rnd. [60 sts]

**Rnd 2:** (MC) ch 1, *sc 1, (CC) sc 3, (MC) sc 1, (CC) sc 1, (MC) sc 3, (CC) sc 1, (MC) sc 1, (CC) sc 3, (MC) sc 1, repeat from * around, join with sl st to ch 1 at beginning of rnd. [60 sts]

**Rnd 3:** (MC) ch 1, *sc 2, (CC) sc 1, (MC) sc 2, (CC) sc 2, (MC) sc 1, (CC) sc 2, (MC) sc 2, (CC) sc 1, (MC) sc 2, repeat from * around, join with sl st to ch 1 at beginning of rnd. [60 sts]

**Rnd 4:** (MC) ch 1, *sc 4, (CC) sc 3, (MC) sc 1, (CC) sc 3, (MC) sc 4, repeat from * around, join with sl st to ch 1 at beginning of rnd. [60 sts]

**Rnd 5:** (MC) ch 1, *sc 2, (CC) sc 3, (MC) sc 1, (CC) sc 1, (MC) sc 1, (CC) sc 1, (MC) sc 1, (CC) sc 3, (MC) sc 2, repeat from * around, join with sl st to ch 1 at beginning of rnd. [60 sts]

**Rnd 6:** (MC) ch 1, *sc 3, (CC) sc 3, (MC) sc 1, (CC) sc 1, (MC) sc 1, (CC) sc 3, (MC) sc 3, repeat from * around, join with sl st to ch 1 at beginning of rnd. [60 sts]

**Rnd 7:** (MC) ch 1, *sc 6, (CC) sc 3, (MC) sc 6, repeat from * around, join with sl st to ch 1 at beginning of rnd. [60 sts]

**Rnd 8:** (MC) ch 1, *sc 3, (CC) sc 3, (MC) sc 1, (CC) sc 1, (MC) sc 1, (CC) sc 3, (MC) sc 3, repeat from * around, join with sl st to ch 1 at beginning of rnd. [60 sts]

**Rnd 9:** (MC) ch 1, *sc 2, (CC) sc 3, (MC) sc 1, (CC) sc 1, (MC) sc 1, (CC) sc 1, (MC) sc 1, (CC) sc 3, (MC) sc 2, repeat from * around, join with sl st to ch 1 at beginning of rnd. [60 sts]

**Rnd 10:** (MC) ch 1, *sc 4, (CC) sc 3, (MC) sc 1, (CC) sc 3, (MC) sc 4, repeat from * around, join with sl st to ch 1 at beginning of rnd. [60 sts]

**Rnd 11:** (MC) ch 1, *sc 2, (CC) sc 1, (MC) sc 2, (CC) sc 2, (MC) sc 1, (CC) sc 2, (MC) sc 2, (CC) sc 1, (MC) sc 2, repeat from * around, join with sl st to ch 1 at beginning of rnd. [60 sts]

**Rnd 12:** (MC) ch 1, *sc 1, (CC) sc 3, (MC) sc 1, (CC) sc 1, (MC) sc 3, (CC) sc 1, (MC) sc 1, (CC) sc 3, (MC) sc 1, repeat from * around, join with sl st to ch 1 at beginning of rnd. [60 sts]

# Falling Snowflakes Hat (Continued)

**Rnd 13:** (MC) ch 1, *sc 2, (CC) sc 1, (MC) sc 9, (CC) sc 1, (MC) sc 2, repeat from * around, join with sl st to ch 1 at beginning of rnd. [60 sts]

Fasten off the CC, continue the rest of the hat with the MC only.

**Rnds 14 through 17:** (MC) ch 1, sc around, join with sl st to ch 1 at beginning of rnd. [60 sts]

Fasten off, leaving a long tail for sewing closed the top of the hat.

To close up the hat, thread the long tail through a yarn needle and sew a basting stitch (see page 21) around the top of the hat, then pull closed. Fasten off once the hat is closed and weave in the ends.

## Attaching a Pom-Pom (Optional)

If you would like to add a faux fur pom-pom, as pictured in the sample, here is how you can do it. Position the pom-pom at the top of the hat, over the hole where you closed up the hat. Sew the pom-pom on top using an embroidery needle and thread, or if it has a snap closure position it on there and secure it. You can also make a pom-pom from yarn using a pom-pom maker and sew it in the same position.

*Can you tell that I like snowflakes? Since it's one of my favorite motifs to use, I thought it would be perfect to do while practicing fair isle crochet worked flat. It's inspired by the crisp winter mornings right after a snowfall. This is the first project where you'll be doing fair isle crochet both worked flat and using the waistcoat stitch. How exciting, so many fun things to try!*

# Winter's Breath Scarf

## Pattern Level: Intermediate

**Gauge:** 4" x 4" (10 x 10 cm) square = 14 waistcoat st x 18 rows

**Measurements:**

- 9" (23 cm) wide x 71" (180 cm) long

**Hook:** US K/10.5 6.5mm

**Yarn:** Lion Brand Basic Stitch Premium (Yarn Weight 4 Medium, 219 yds [200 m], 3.5 oz [100 g], 100 percent acrylic) in two colors:

- Plum (MC)
- Cream (CC)

**Approximate Yarn Yardage:**

MC = 657 yds (601 m)

CC = 219 yds (200 m)

**Abbreviations:**

ch = chain

st(s) = stitch(es)

sc = single crochet

ws = waistcoat stitch (see pages 112–113 for detailed instructions on how to do this stitch)

MC = main color

CC = contrast color

# Winter's Breath Scarf (Continued)

## Starting Rows

Starting with MC, ch 249.

**Row 1:** starting in second ch from hook, sc 248.

**Rows 2 through 9:** ch 1, turn, ws 248.

## Scarf Colorwork

The next row is going to begin the colorwork for the scarf. We'll be joining the CC in this row and will carry it across the row to do all of the colorwork using the fair isle technique. The rows will start with new row numbers so that it will be easier to follow along with the chart. Each row number for the colorwork corresponds to the same row number on the chart.

**Row 1:** (MC) ch 1 (ch 1 at the beginning of the row does not count as a st throughout the rest of the pattern), turn, *ws 1, (CC) ws 1, (MC) ws 2, (CC) ws 1, (MC) ws 8, (CC) ws 1, (MC) ws 3, (CC) ws 1, (MC) ws 8, (CC) ws 1, (MC) ws 2, (CC) ws 1, (MC) ws 1, repeat from * 7 more times. [248 sts]

**Row 2:** (MC) ch 1, turn, *ws 2, (CC) ws 2, (MC) ws 9, (CC) ws 2, (MC) ws 1, (CC) ws 2, (MC) ws 9, (CC) ws 2, (MC) ws 2, repeat from * 7 more times. [248 sts]

**Row 3:** (MC) ch 1, turn, *ws 2, (CC) ws 2, (MC) ws 7, (CC) ws 1, (MC) ws 1, (CC) ws 1, (MC) ws 1, (CC) ws 1, (MC) ws 1, (CC) ws 1, (MC) ws 1, (CC) ws 1, (MC) ws 7, (CC) ws 2, (MC) ws 2, repeat from * 7 more times. [248 sts]

### Pro Tip

As you use the waistcoat stitch while working flat, it will look different than when worked in the round. It still captures the knit-like texture, but the stitches will look slightly different.

**Row 4:** (MC) ch 1, turn, *ws 1, (CC) ws 1, (MC) ws 2, (CC) ws 1, (MC) ws 5, (CC) ws 1, (MC) ws 1, (CC) ws 2, (MC) ws 3, (CC) ws 2, (MC) ws 1, (CC) ws 1, (MC) ws 5, (CC) ws 1, (MC) ws 2, (CC) ws 1, (MC) ws 1, repeat from * 7 more times. [248 sts]

**Row 5:** (MC) ch 1, turn, *ws 9, (CC) ws 1, (MC) ws 3, (CC) ws 1, (MC) ws 3, (CC) ws 1, (MC) ws 3, (CC) ws 1, (MC) ws 9, repeat from * 7 more times. [248 sts]

# Winter's Breath Scarf (Continued)

**Row 9:** (MC) ch 1, turn, *ws 7, (CC) ws 1, (MC) ws 1, (CC) ws 1, (MC) ws 3, (CC) ws 1, (MC) ws 3, (CC) ws 1, (MC) ws 3, (CC) ws 1, (MC) ws 1, (CC) ws 1, (MC) ws 7, repeat from * 7 more times. [248 sts]

> **Pro Tip**
>
> Having trouble with your stitches blending together when the colors aren't directly stacked on top of each other over two rows? Go through the back post of the waistcoat stitch when you're doing the colored stitch on the second row and it will help the two colored stitches blend together.

**Row 10:** (MC) ch 1, turn, *ws 4, (CC) ws 6, (MC) ws 2, (CC) ws 7, (MC) ws 2, (CC) ws 6, (MC) ws 4, repeat from * 7 more times. [248 sts]

**Row 11:** (MC) ch 1, turn, *ws 5, (CC) ws 1, (MC) ws 3, (CC) ws 1, (MC) ws 1, (CC) ws 1, (MC) ws 1, (CC) ws 1, (MC) ws 3, (CC) ws 1, (MC) ws 1, (CC) ws 1, (MC) ws 1, (CC) ws 1, (MC) ws 3, (CC) ws 1, (MC) ws 5, repeat from * 7 more times. [248 sts]

**Row 6:** (MC) ch 1, turn, *ws 2, (CC) ws 1, (MC) ws 5, (CC) ws 15, (MC) ws 5, (CC) ws 1, (MC) ws 2, repeat from * 7 more times. [248 sts]

**Row 7:** (MC) ch 1, turn, *ws 1, (CC) ws 3, (MC) ws 3, (CC) ws 1, (MC) ws 1, (CC) ws 1, (MC) ws 5, (CC) ws 1, (MC) ws 5, (CC) ws 1, (MC) ws 1, (CC) ws 1, (MC) ws 3, (CC) ws 3, (MC) ws 1, repeat from * 7 more times. [248 sts]

**Row 8:** (MC) ch 1, turn, *ws 2, (CC) ws 1, (MC) ws 3, (CC) ws 1, (MC) ws 2, (CC) ws 1, (MC) ws 4, (CC) ws 1, (MC) ws 1, (CC) ws 1, (MC) ws 4, (CC) ws 1, (MC) ws 2, (CC) ws 1, (MC) ws 3, (CC) ws 1, (MC) ws 2, repeat from * 7 more times. [248 sts]

**Row 12:** (MC) ch 1, turn, *ws 6, (CC) ws 1, (MC) ws 2, (CC) ws 2, (MC) ws 2, (CC) ws 1, (MC) ws 1, (CC) ws 1, (MC) ws 1, (CC) ws 1, (MC) ws 2, (CC) ws 2, (MC) ws 2, (CC) ws 1, (MC) ws 6, repeat from * 7 more times. [248 sts]

**Row 13:** (MC) ch 1, turn, *ws 5, (CC) ws 1, (MC) ws 3, (CC) ws 1, (MC) ws 1, (CC) ws 1, (MC) ws 1, (CC) ws 1, (MC) ws 3, (CC) ws 1, (MC) ws 1, (CC) ws 1, (MC) ws 1, (CC) ws 1, (MC) ws 3, (CC) ws 1, (MC) ws 5, repeat from * 7 more times. [248 sts]

**Row 14:** (MC) ch 1, turn, *ws 4, (CC) ws 6, (MC) ws 2, (CC) ws 7, (MC) ws 2, (CC) ws 6, (MC) ws 4, repeat from * 7 more times. [248 sts]

**Row 15:** (MC) ch 1, turn, *ws 7, (CC) ws 1, (MC) ws 1, (CC) ws 1, (MC) ws 3, (CC) ws 1, (MC) ws 3, (CC) ws 1, (MC) ws 3, (CC) ws 1, (MC) ws 1, (CC) ws 1, (MC) ws 7, repeat from * 7 more times. [248 sts]

**Row 16:** (MC) ch 1, turn, *ws 2, (CC) ws 1, (MC) ws 3, (CC) ws 1, (MC) ws 2, (CC) ws 1, (MC) ws 4, (CC) ws 1, (MC) ws 1, (CC) ws 1, (MC) ws 4, (CC) ws 1, (MC) ws 2, (CC) ws 1, (MC) ws 3, (CC) ws 1, (MC) ws 2, repeat from * 7 more times. [248 sts]

**Row 17:** (MC) ch 1, turn, *ws 1, (CC) ws 3, (MC) ws 3, (CC) ws 1, (MC) ws 1, (CC) ws 1, (MC) ws 5, (CC) ws 1, (MC) ws 5, (CC) ws 1, (MC) ws 1, (CC) ws 1, (MC) ws 3, (CC) ws 3, (MC) ws 1, repeat from * 7 more times. [248 sts]

**Row 18:** (MC) ch 1, turn, *ws 2, (CC) ws 1, (MC) ws 5, (CC) ws 15, (MC) ws 5, (CC) ws 1, (MC) ws 2, repeat from * 7 more times. [248 sts]

**Row 19:** (MC) ch 1, turn, *ws 9, (CC) ws 1, (MC) ws 3, (CC) ws 1, (MC) ws 3, (CC) ws 1, (MC) ws 3, (CC) ws 1, (MC) ws 9, repeat from * 7 more times. [248 sts]

**Row 20:** (MC) ch 1, turn, *ws 1, (CC) ws 1, (MC) ws 2, (CC) ws 1, (MC) ws 5, (CC) ws 1, (MC) ws 1, (CC) ws 2, (MC) ws 3, (CC) ws 2, (MC) ws 1, (CC) ws 1, (MC) ws 5, (CC) ws 1, (MC) ws 2, (CC) ws 1, (MC) ws 1, repeat from * 7 more times. [248 sts]

**Row 21:** (MC) ch 1, turn, *ws 2, (CC) ws 2, (MC) ws 7, (CC) ws 1, (MC) ws 1, (CC) ws 1, (MC) ws 1, (CC) ws 1, (MC) ws 1, (CC) ws 1, (MC) ws 1, (CC) ws 1, (MC) ws 7, (CC) ws 2, (MC) ws 2, repeat from * 7 more times. [248 sts]

**Row 22:** (MC) ch 1, turn, *ws 2, (CC) ws 2, (MC) ws 9, (CC) ws 2, (MC) ws 1, (CC) ws 2, (MC) ws 9, (CC) ws 2, (MC) ws 2, repeat from * 7 more times. [248 sts]

**Row 23:** (MC) ch 1, turn, *ws 1, (CC) ws 1, (MC) ws 2, (CC) ws 1, (MC) ws 8, (CC) ws 1, (MC) ws 3, (CC) ws 1, (MC) ws 8, (CC) ws 1, (MC) ws 2, (CC) ws 1, (MC) ws 1, repeat from * 7 more times. [248 sts]

Fasten off the CC, and continue with only the MC.

## Finishing Rows

**Rows 24 through 31:** (MC) ch 1, turn, ws across. [248 sts]

Fasten off and weave in the ends.

# Winter's Breath Scarf (Continued)

## Chart

■ Main Color

□ Contrast Color

For chart notes and how to read a chart, see pages 15-17.

*The Dancing Leaves Mittens were inspired by the changing fall leaves. I love all of the deep color tones and beauty of the leaves. This pattern is the first one where you'll learn how to do the waistcoat stitch in the round, which is my favorite way to use it. I'll walk you through carrying the yarn and doing the different steps of this technique. You'll definitely want to show off these mittens during the cold months.*

# Dancing Leaves Mittens

## Pattern Level: Intermediate

**Gauge for Body of Mitten:** 4" x 4" (10 x 10 cm) square = 14 ws x 17 rows

**Gauge for Wrist Ribbing:** 4" x 4" (10 x 10 cm) square (worked in alternating rows of blo and flo) = 13 hdc x 8 rows

**Mitten Measurements:**

- Wrist measurement = 7.5" (19 cm)
- Hand measurement = 8" (20 cm)
- Length = 7.5" (19 cm)

**Hook:** US K/10.5 6.5mm

**Yarn:** Lion Brand Heartland (Yarn Weight 4 Medium, 251 yds [230 m], 5 oz [142 g], 100 percent acrylic) in two colors:

- Kings Canyon (MC)
- Yosemite (CC)

**Approximate Yarn Yardage:**

- MC = 70 yds (64 m)
- CC = 30 yds (27 m)

**Extra Materials:**

Yarn needle

**Abbreviations:**

ch = chain

st(s) = stitch(es)

sc = single crochet

hdc = half double crochet

ws = waistcoat stitch (see pages 112–113 for detailed instructions on how to do this stitch)

rnd = round

sl st = slip stitch

sk = skip

MC = main color

CC = contrast color

dec = decrease (single crochet two together)

# Dancing Leaves Mittens (Continued)

## Chart

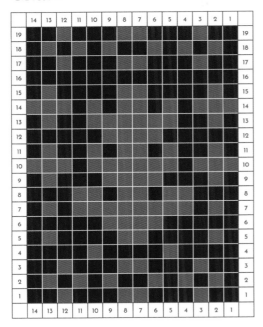

| | 14 | 13 | 12 | 11 | 10 | 9 | 8 | 7 | 6 | 5 | 4 | 3 | 2 | 1 | |
|---|---|---|---|---|---|---|---|---|---|---|---|---|---|---|---|

Main Color

Contrast Color

For chart notes and how to read a chart, see pages 15–17.

## How to Follow the Pattern

The process for making these mittens begins with doing the wrist ribbing, then moving on to the body of the mittens. The wrist ribbing is the same for each hand, and then within the directions for the body of the mittens, it includes instructions specific to each hand. After the body, you'll follow the instructions for the thumbs. So you'll repeat the whole process of ribbing, body, then thumb for each hand.

## Wrist Ribbing

Starting with CC, ch 6.

**Row 1:** starting in third ch from hook, hdc 4. [4 sts]

**Row 2:** ch 2 (ch 2 at the beginning of the row does not count as a st throughout the rest of the ribbing), turn, hdc across in the blo. [4 sts]

**Row 3:** ch 2, turn, hdc across in the flo. [4 sts]

For the next ten rows, alternate between repeating rows 2 and 3.

Once you're done with those rows, join the two ends of your wrist ribbing right sides together with a sl st. Turn it right-side out, and then you'll move on to the body of the mittens.

## Body of Mittens

To switch to the main color, do your first ch st with the new color. Do not fasten off CC. We will be using it after the first two rnds. The first round sets up the base of the ws that we'll be using to make the rest of the mittens.

**Rnd 1:** ch 1 (ch 1 at the beginning of the rnd does not count as a st throughout the rest of the pattern), sc 28 around the top of the wrist ribbing (working approximately 2 sts in each row end of wrist ribbing), join with sl st to the ch 1 at the beginning of the rnd. [28 sts]

# Dancing Leaves Mittens (Continued)

**Rnd 2:** ch 1, ws around, join with sl st to ch 1 at the beginning of the rnd. [28 sts]

Starting in the next rnd, you will use the chart. Rnd 3 corresponds to row 1 of the chart, rnd 4 to row 2, and so on. Carry the CC around using floats.

**Rnd 3 (starts first row of chart):** (MC) ch 1, ws 7, begin using chart, ws 2, join (CC) to mitten and ws 1, (MC) ws 3, (CC) ws 2, (MC) ws 3, (CC) ws 1, (MC) ws 2. You should reach the end of the colorwork chart, if using. (MC) ws 7, join with sl st to ch 1 at beginning of rnd. [28 sts]

**Rnd 4:** (MC) ch 1, ws 7, begin using chart, ws 1, (CC) ws 1, (MC) ws 1, (CC) ws 1, (MC) ws 1, (CC) ws 1, (MC) ws 2, (CC) ws 1, (MC) ws 1, (CC) ws 1, (MC) ws 1, (CC) ws 1, (MC) ws 1. You should reach the end of the colorwork chart, if using. (MC) ws 7, join with sl st to ch 1 at beginning of rnd. [28 sts]

**Rnd 5:** (MC) ch 1, ws 7, begin using chart, ws 2, (CC) ws 1, (MC) ws 3, (CC) ws 2, (MC) ws 3, (CC) ws 1, (MC) ws 2. You should reach the end of the colorwork chart, if using. (MC) ws 7, join with sl st to ch 1 at beginning of rnd. [28 sts]

For next three rnds, follow the instructions for the hand you are working on.

## Right Hand

**Rnd 6:** (MC) ch 1, ws 7, begin using chart, ws 4, (CC) ws 1, (MC) ws 4, (CC) ws 1, (MC) ws 4. You should reach the end of the colorwork chart, if using. (MC) ch 5, sk 5 sts to form the thumb hole (see photo 1), starting in the next st ws 2, join with sl st to ch 1 at beginning of rnd. [28 sts]

**Rnd 7:** (MC) ch 1, ws 7, begin using chart, ws 1, (CC) ws 1, (MC) ws 4, (CC) ws 2, (MC) ws 4, (CC) ws 1, (MC) ws 1. You should reach the end of the colorwork chart, if using. (MC) sc 5 through the five chains from the thumb hole and crochet around the strand of CC1 that stretched across the thumb hole (see photo 2), ws 2, join with sl st to ch 1 at beginning of rnd. [28 sts]

**Rnd 8:** (MC) ch 1, ws 7, begin using chart, ws 5, (CC) ws 4, (MC) ws 5. You should reach the end of the colorwork chart, if using. (MC) ws 7 including through the sc sts from the previous rnd, join with sl st to ch 1 at beginning of rnd. [28 sts]

Skip to Rnd 9 to continue with the rest of the mitten.

## Left Hand

**Rnd 6:** (MC) ch 1, ws 2, ch 5, sk 5 sts to form the thumb hole, begin using chart, ws 4, (CC) ws 1, (MC) ws 4, (CC) ws 1, (MC) ws 4. You should reach the end of the colorwork chart, if using. (MC) ws 7, join with sl st to ch 1 at beginning of rnd. [28 sts]

**Rnd 7:** (MC) ch 1, ws 7, sc 5 through the five chains from the thumb hole and crochet around the strand of CC1 that stretched across the thumb hole, begin using chart, ws 1, (CC) ws 1, (MC) ws 4, (CC) ws 2, (MC) ws 4, (CC) ws 1, (MC) ws 1. You should reach the end of the colorwork chart, if using. (MC) ws 2, join with sl st to ch 1 at beginning of rnd. [28 sts]

**Rnd 8:** (MC) ch 1, ws 7 including through the sc sts from the previous rnd, begin using chart, ws 5, (CC) ws 4, (MC) ws 5. You should reach the end of the colorwork chart, if using. (MC) ws 7, join with sl st to ch 1 at beginning of rnd. [28 sts]

Continue the rest of the mitten following the instructions starting at Rnd 9 below.

## Both Hands

**Rnd 9:** (MC) ch 1, ws 7, begin using chart, ws 1, (CC) ws 1, (MC) ws 1, (CC) ws 8, (MC) ws 1, (CC) ws 1, (MC) ws 1. You should reach the end of the colorwork chart, if using. (MC) ws 7, join with sl st to ch 1 at beginning of rnd. [28 sts]

**Rnd 10:** (MC) ch 1, ws 7, begin using chart, ws 3, (CC) ws 2, (MC) ws 1, (CC) ws 2, (MC) ws 1, (CC) ws 2, (MC) ws 3. You should reach the end of the colorwork chart, if using. (MC) ws 7, join with sl st to ch 1 at beginning of rnd. [28 sts]

**Rnd 11:** (MC) ch 1, ws 7, begin using chart, ws 1, (CC) ws 1, (MC) ws 3, (CC) ws 4, (MC) ws 3, (CC) ws 1, (MC) ws 1. You should reach the end of the colorwork chart, if using. (MC) ws 7, join with sl st to ch 1 at beginning of rnd. [28 sts]

**Rnd 12:** (MC) ch 1, ws 7, begin using chart, ws 3, (MC) ws 1, (CC) ws 6, (MC) ws 1, (CC) ws 3. You should reach the end of the colorwork chart, if using. (MC) ws 7, join with sl st to ch 1 at beginning of rnd. [28 sts]

**Rnd 13:** (MC) ch 1, ws 7, begin using chart, ws 1, (CC) ws 1, (MC) ws 2, (CC) ws 1, (MC) ws 1, (CC) ws 2, (MC) ws 1, (CC) ws 1, (MC) ws 2, (CC) ws 1, (MC) ws 1. You should reach the end of the colorwork chart, if using. (MC) ws 7, join with sl st to ch 1 at beginning of rnd. [28 sts]

# Dancing Leaves Mittens (Continued)

**Rnd 14:** (MC) ch 1, ws 7, begin using chart, ws 5, (CC) ws 4, (MC) ws 5. You should reach the end of the colorwork chart, if using. (MC) ws 7, join with sl st to ch 1 at beginning of rnd. [28 sts]

**Rnd 15:** (MC) ch 1, ws 7, begin using chart, ws 1, (CC) ws 1, (MC) ws 2, (CC) ws 6, (MC) ws 2, (CC) ws 1, (MC) ws 1. You should reach the end of the colorwork chart, if using. (MC) ws 7, join with sl st to ch 1 at beginning of rnd. [28 sts]

**Rnd 16:** (CC) ch 1, ws 7, begin using chart, ws 3, (MC) ws 1, (CC) ws 1, (MC) ws 1, (CC) ws 2, (MC) ws 1, (CC) ws 1, (MC) ws 1, (CC) ws 3. You should reach the end of the colorwork chart, if using. (MC) ws 7, join with sl st to ch 1 at beginning of rnd. [28 sts]

**Rnd 17:** (MC) ch 1, ws 7, begin using chart, ws 1, (CC) ws 1, (MC) ws 4, (CC) ws 2, (MC) ws 4, (CC) ws 1, (MC) ws 1. You should reach the end of the colorwork chart, if using. (MC) ws 7, join with sl st to ch 1 at beginning of rnd. [28 sts]

**Rnd 18:** (MC) ch 1, ws around, join with sl st to ch 1 at beginning of rnd. [28 sts]

**Rnd 19:** (MC) ch 1, ws 7, begin using chart, ws 2, (CC) ws 1, (MC) ws 3, (CC) ws 2, (MC) ws 3, (CC) ws 1, (MC) ws 2. You should reach the end of the colorwork chart, if using. (MC) ws 7, join with sl st to ch 1 at beginning of rnd. [28 sts]

**Rnd 20:** (MC) ch 1, ws 7, begin using chart, ws 1, (CC) ws 1, (MC) ws 1, (CC) ws 1, (MC) ws 1, (CC) ws 1, (MC) ws 2, (CC) ws 1, (MC) ws 1, (CC) ws 1, (MC) ws 1, (CC) ws 1, (MC) ws 1. You should reach the end of the colorwork chart, if using. (MC) ws 7, join with sl st to ch 1 at beginning of rnd. [28 sts]

**Rnd 21:** (MC) ch 1, ws 7, begin using chart, ws 2, (CC) ws 1, (MC) ws 3, (CC) ws 2, (MC) ws 3, (CC) ws 1, (MC) ws 2. You should reach the end of the colorwork chart, if using. (MC) ws 7, join with sl st to ch 1 at beginning of rnd. [28 sts]

**Rnd 22:** (MC) ch 1, ws around, join with sl st to ch 1 at beginning of rnd. [28 sts]

**Rnd 23:** (MC) ch 1, *ws 2, dec, repeat from * around, join with sl st to ch 1 at beginning of rnd. [21 sts]

**Rnd 24:** (MC) ch 1, ws around, join with sl st to ch 1 at beginning of rnd. [21 sts]

**Rnd 25:** (MC) ch 1, *ws 1, dec, repeat from * around, join with sl st to ch 1 at beginning of rnd. [14 sts]

**Rnd 26:** (MC) ch 1, ws around, join with sl st to ch 1 at beginning of rnd.

**Rnd 27:** (MC) ch 1, dec 7, join with sl st to ch 1 at beginning of rnd. [7 sts]

Using a basting st (see page 21), sew along the top of the mittens and pull to tighten and close up. Then fasten off and weave in the ends.

## Thumb

Using the MC, join yarn with a sl st to either the first or last st you skipped when forming the thumb hole.

**Rnd 1:** ch 1, ws 10 around, join with sl st to ch 1 at beginning of rnd. [10 sts]

**Rnds 2 through 6:** ch 1, ws around, join with sl st to ch 1 at beginning of rnd. [10 sts]

**Rnd 7:** ch 1, dec 5, join with sl st to ch 1 at beginning of rnd. [5 sts]

Fasten off, leaving a small tail to sew the top closed.

Using a basting st (see page 21), close the top of the thumb up, then fasten off and weave in the ends.

## Attaching a Pom-Pom (Optional)

If you would like to add a faux fur pom-pom, as pictured in the sample, here is how you can do it. Position the pom-pom at the top of the hat, over the hole where you closed up the hat. Sew the pom-pom on top using an embroidery needle and thread, or if it has a snap closure position it on there and secure it. You can also make a pom-pom from yarn using a pom-pom maker and sew it in the same position.

# Dancing Leaves Beanie

## Pattern Level: Beginner

**Gauge for Body of Hat:** 4″ x 4″ (10 x 10 cm) square = 14 ws x 17 rows

**Gauge for Brim:** 4″ x 4″ (10 x 10 cm) square (worked in alternating rows of blo and flo) = 13 hdc x 8 rows

**Finished Hat Dimensions:**
- Height = 8″ (20 cm) tall
- Circumference = 22.9″ (58 cm)

**Hook:** US K/10.5 6.5mm

**Yarn:** Lion Brand Heartland (Yarn Weight 4 Medium, 251 yds [230 m], 5 oz [142 g], 100 percent acrylic) in two colors:
- Kings Canyon (MC)
- Yosemite (CC)

**Approximate Yarn Yardage:**
MC = 100 yds (92 m)
CC = 80 yds (73 m)

**Extra Materials:**
Yarn needle

**Abbreviations:**

ch = chain

sc = single crochet

hdc = half double crochet

blo = back loops only

flo = front loops only

st(s) = stitch(es)

sl st = slip stitch

rnd = round

ws = waistcoat stitch (see pages 112–113 for tutorial on how to do this stitch)

MC = main color

CC = contrast color

# Dancing Leaves Beanie (Continued)

## Chart

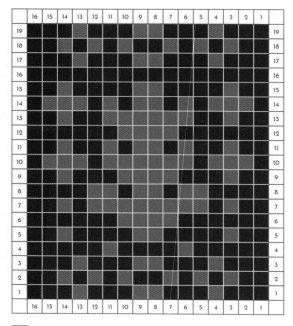

| ■ | Main Color |
| ■ | Contrast Color |

For chart notes and how to read a chart, see pages 15–17.

## Brim

Starting with the CC, ch 8.

**Row 1:** starting in third ch from hook, hdc 6. [6 sts]

**Row 2:** ch 2 (ch 2 at the beginning of the row does not count as a st throughout the rest of the brim), turn, hdc across in the blo. [6 sts]

**Row 3:** ch 2, turn, hdc across in the flo. [6 sts]

For the next 37 rows, alternate between repeating rows 2 and 3 for a total of 40 rows from beginning.

Once you're done with those rows, join the two ends of your brim right sides together with a sl st. Turn it right-side out, and then move on to the body of the hat.

## Body of Hat

To switch to the MC, do your first ch st with the new color. Do not fasten off the CC. We will be using it after the first two rnds. The first round sets up the base of the ws that we'll be using to make the rest of the hat.

**Rnd 1:** ch 1 (ch 1 at the beginning of the rnd does not count as a st throughout the rest of the pattern), sc 80 around the top of the brim of the beanie (working approximately 2 sts in each row end of brim), join with sl st to the ch 1 at the beginning of the rnd. [80 sts]

The next rnd will be the first rnd of ws. Please see pages 15–17 for how to do the ws.

**Rnd 2:** ch 1, ws around, join with sl st to ch 1 at beginning of rnd. [80 sts]

**Rnd 3 (starts first row of chart):** (MC), ch 1, *ws 3, (CC) ws 1, (MC) ws 3, (CC) ws 2, (MC) ws 3, (CC) ws 1, (MC) ws 3, repeat from * 4 more times, join with sl st to ch 1 at beginning of rnd. [80 sts]

**Rnd 4:** (MC) ch 1, *ws 2, [(CC) ws 1, (MC) ws 1] 3 times, [(MC) ws 1, (CC) ws 1] 3 times, (MC) ws 2, repeat from * 4 more times, join with sl st to ch 1 at beginning of rnd. [80 sts]

**Rnd 5:** (MC) ch 1, *ws 3, (CC) ws 1, (MC) ws 3, (CC) ws 2, (MC) ws 3, (CC) ws 1, (MC) ws 3, repeat from * 4 more times, join with sl st to ch 1 at beginning of rnd. [80 sts]

**Rnd 6:** (MC) ch 1, *ws 5, (CC) ws 1, (MC) ws 4, (CC) ws 1, (MC) ws 5, repeat from * 4 more times, join with sl st to ch 1 at beginning of rnd. [80 sts]

**Rnd 7:** (MC) ch 1, *ws 2, (CC) ws 1, (MC) ws 4, (CC) ws 2, (MC) ws 4, (CC) ws 1, (MC) ws 2, repeat from * 4 more times, join with sl st to ch 1 at beginning of rnd. [80 sts]

**Rnd 8:** (MC) ch 1, *ws 6, (CC) ws 4, (MC) ws 6, repeat from * 4 more times, join with sl st to ch 1 at beginning of rnd. [80 sts]

**Rnd 9:** (MC) ch 1, *ws 2, (CC) ws 1, (MC) ws 1, (CC) ws 8, (MC) ws 1, (CC) ws 1, (MC) ws 2, repeat from * 4 more times, join with sl st to ch 1 at beginning of rnd. [80 sts]

**Rnd 10:** (MC) ch 1, *ws 4, (CC) ws 2, (MC) ws 1, (CC) ws 2, (MC) ws 1, (CC) ws 2, (MC) ws 4, repeat from * 4 more times, join with sl st to ch 1 at beginning of rnd. [80 sts]

**Rnd 11:** (MC) ch 1, *ws 2, (CC) ws 1, (MC) ws 3, (CC) ws 4, (MC) ws 3, (CC) ws 1, (MC) ws 2, repeat from * 4 more times, join with sl st to ch 1 at beginning of rnd. [80 sts]

**Rnd 12:** (CC) ch 1, *ws 1, (CC) ws 3, (MC) ws 1, (CC) ws 6, (MC) ws 1, (CC) ws 3, (MC) ws 1, repeat from * 4 more times, join with sl st to ch 1 at beginning of rnd. [80 sts]

**Rnd 13:** (MC) ch 1, *ws 2, (CC) ws 1, (MC) ws 2, (CC) ws 1, (MC) ws 1, (CC) ws 2, (MC) ws 1, (CC) ws 1, (MC) ws 2, (CC) ws 1, (MC) ws 2, repeat from * 4 more times, join with sl st to ch 1 at beginning of rnd. [80 sts]

**Rnd 14:** (MC) ch 1, *ws 6, (CC) ws 4, (MC) ws 6, repeat from * 4 more times, join with sl st to ch 1 at beginning of rnd. [80 sts]

# Dancing Leaves Beanie (Continued)

**Rnd 18:** (MC) ch 1, ws around, join with sl st to ch 1 at beginning of rnd. [80 sts]

**Rnd 19:** (MC) ch 1, *ws 3, (CC) ws 1, (MC) ws 3, (CC) ws 2, (MC) ws 3, (CC) ws 1, (MC) ws 3, repeat from * 4 more times, join with sl st to ch 1 at beginning of rnd. [80 sts]

**Rnd 20:** (MC) ch 1, *ws 2, (CC) ws 1, (MC) ws 1, (CC) ws 1, (MC) ws 1, (CC) ws 1, (MC) ws 2, (CC) ws 1, (MC) ws 1, (CC) ws 1, (MC) ws 1, (CC) ws 1, (MC) ws 2, repeat from * 4 more times, join with sl st to ch 1 at beginning of rnd. [80 sts]

**Rnd 21:** (MC) ch 1, *ws 3, (CC) ws 1, (MC) ws 3, (CC) ws 2, (MC) ws 3, (CC) ws 1, (MC) ws 3, repeat from * 4 more times, join with sl st to ch 1 at beginning of rnd. [80 sts]

**Next five rnds:** (MC) ch 1, ws around, join with sl st to ch 1 at beginning of rnd. [80 sts]

Fasten off, leaving a long tail for sewing the hat closed.

To close up the hat, thread the long tail through a yarn needle and sew a basting stitch (see page 21) around the top of the hat, then pull closed. Fasten off once hat is closed, and weave in the ends.

## Attaching a Pom-Pom (Optional)

If you would like to add a faux fur pom-pom, as pictured in the sample, here is how you can do it. Position the pom-pom at the top of the hat, over the hole where you closed up the hat. Sew the pom-pom on top using an embroidery needle and thread, or if it has a snap closure position it on there and secure it. You can also make a pom-pom from yarn using a pom-pom maker and sew it in the same position.

**Rnd 15:** (MC) ch 1, *ws 2, (CC) ws 1, (MC) ws 2, (CC) ws 6, (MC) ws 2, (CC) ws 1, (MC) ws 2, repeat from * 4 more times, join with sl st to ch 1 at beginning of rnd. [80 sts]

**Rnd 16:** (CC) ch 1, *ws 1, (CC) ws 3, (MC) ws 1, (CC) ws 1, (MC) ws 1, (CC) ws 2, (MC) ws 1, (CC) ws 1, (MC) ws 1, (CC) ws 3, (MC) ws 1, repeat from * 4 more times, join with sl st to ch 1 at beginning of rnd. [80 sts]

**Rnd 17:** (MC) ch 1, *ws 2, (CC) ws 1, (MC) ws 4, (CC) ws 2, (MC) ws 4, (CC) ws 1, (MC) ws 2, repeat from * 4 more times, join with sl st to ch 1 at beginning of rnd. [80 sts]

*The Falling Snowflakes Sweater was inspired by the first snow of winter and classic yoke sweaters. This sweater will introduce you to the wonderful world of circular yoke sweaters. You'll learn how to do a fair isle crochet garment in the round, and continue using the techniques for fair isle crochet in the round we learned with the Falling Snowflakes Hat from this chapter (page 115).*

# Falling Snowflakes Sweater

## Pattern Level: Intermediate

**Gauge:** 4" x 4" (10 x 10 cm) square = 11 sc x 12 Rnds

**Sizes:** XS (S, M, L, XL, 2X, 3X, 4X, 5X)

**Finished Bust Measurements:**
- 36 (40, 44, 47, 55, 55, 62, 69, 73)"
- 92 (102, 112, 120, 140, 140, 158, 175, 186) cm

**Waist Measurement:**
- 29 (33, 36, 40, 47, 47, 55, 62, 65)"
- 74 (84, 92, 102, 120, 120, 140, 158, 165) cm

**Finished Arm Length:**
- 16 (17, 17, 18, 18, 18, 18, 19, 19)"
- 41 (43, 43, 46, 46, 46, 46, 48, 48) cm

**Finished Sweater Length:**
- 23 (24, 25, 26, 27, 28, 29, 30, 31)"
- 58 (61, 64, 66, 69, 71, 74, 76, 79) cm

**Hook:** US L/11 8mm

**Yarn:** Lion Brand Color Made Easy (Yarn Weight 5 Bulky, 247 yds [226 m], 7 oz [200 g], 100 percent acrylic) in two colors:
- Kombucha (MC)
- Alabaster (CC)

**Approximate Yarn Yardage:**

MC = 498 (575, 705, 843, 989, 1043, 1205, 1374, 1551) yds (455 [526, 645, 771, 904, 954, 1102, 1256, 1418] m)

CC = 200 yds (183 m) for XS-L, 300 yds (274 m) for XL-5XL

**Abbreviations:**

ch = chain

st(s) = stitch(es)

sc = single crochet

rnd = round

sl st = slip stitch

MC = main color

CC = contrast color

sk = skip

inc = increase

dec = decrease

blo = back loops only

FSC = foundation single crochet

# Falling Snowflakes Sweater (Continued)

## Yoke Sizes XS to L

The ch 1 at the beginning of each rnd does not count as a st. Each rnd corresponds with the same numbered row on the chart.

**Rnd 1:** Starting with MC, FSC 51. Join first and last FSC together with a sl st. The first FSC will no longer count as a stitch. [50 sts]

**Rnd 2:** (CC) ch 1 (ch 1 at the beginning of the rnd does not count as a st throughout the rest of the pattern), working all sts in the blo, *sc 4, inc 1, repeat from * 9 more times, join with sl st to ch 1 at beginning of rnd. [60 sts]

Continue working all sts in the blo, which helps offset slanting in the colorwork.

**Rnd 3:** (CC) ch 1, *sc 2, (MC) sc 1, (CC) sc 2, (MC) inc 1, repeat from * 9 more times, join with sl st to ch 1 at beginning of rnd. [70 sts]

**Rnd 4:** (MC) ch 1, *sc 1, (CC) sc 3, (MC) sc 2, inc 1, repeat from * 9 more times, join with sl st to ch 1 at beginning of rnd. [80 sts]

**Rnd 5:** (MC) ch 1, *sc 7, inc 1, repeat from * 9 more times, join with sl st to ch 1 at beginning of rnd. [90 sts]

**Rnd 6:** (MC) ch 1, *sc 2, (CC) sc 1, (MC) sc 4, (CC) sc 1, (MC) inc 1, repeat from * 9 more times, join with sl st to ch 1 at beginning of rnd. [100 sts]

**Rnd 7:** (MC) ch 1, *sc 1, (CC) sc 3, (MC) sc 2, (CC) sc 3, (MC) inc 1, repeat from * 9 more times, join with sl st to ch 1 at beginning of rnd. [110 sts]

**Rnd 8:** (MC) ch 1, *sc 2, (CC) sc 1, (MC) sc 4, (CC) sc 1, (MC) sc 2, inc 1, repeat from * 9 more times, join with sl st to ch 1 at beginning of rnd. [120 sts]

**Rnd 9:** (MC) ch 1, *sc 11, inc 1, repeat from * 9 more times, join with sl st to ch 1 at beginning of rnd. [130 sts]

**Rnd 10:** (MC) ch 1, *sc 6, (CC) sc 1, (MC) sc 1, (CC) sc 1, (MC) sc 3, inc 1, repeat from * 9 more times, join with sl st to ch 1 at beginning of rnd. [140 sts]

**Rnd 11:** (MC) ch 1, *sc 5, (CC) sc 2, (MC) sc 1, (CC) sc 2, (MC) sc 3, inc 1, repeat from * 9 more times, join with sl st to ch 1 at beginning of rnd. [150 sts]

**Rnd 12** (Last increase rnd for size XS): (MC) ch 1, *sc 3, (CC) sc 4, (MC) sc 1, (CC) sc 4, (MC) sc 2, inc 1, repeat from * 9 more times, join with sl st to ch 1 at beginning of rnd. [160 sts]

From this point on, size XS will no longer be doing an increase at the end of the section of colorwork. Where the increase normally is, there will be an x, followed by the increases for the other sizes. When a size stops increasing, there will be an x to replace the inc. No matter what size you are making, you will keep doing the following rnds to complete the yoke. The colorwork before the increase will have the correct number of sc that you work for your chosen size within the written pattern.

If you are using the chart, mark which row you will stop doing increases on. I recommend drawing a vertical line where you stop increasing on the chart. This way you can still keep using the chart to complete the pattern by doing each stitch up to that line. You can also just use the written pattern if that is easier.

**Rnd 13** (Last increase rnd for size S): (MC) sc 1, (CC) sc 1, (MC) sc 2, (CC) sc 7, (MC) sc 2, (CC) sc 1, (MC) sc 2 (1, 1, 1), inc x (1, 1, 1), repeat from * 9 more times, join with sl st to ch 1 at beginning of rnd. [160 (170, 170, 170) sts]

**Rnd 14** (Last increase rnd for size M): (CC) sc 3, (MC) sc 3, (CC) sc 3, (MC) sc 3, (CC) sc 3, (MC) sc 1 (2, 1, 1), inc x (x, 1, 1), repeat from * 9 more times, join with sl st to ch 1 at beginning of rnd. [160 (170, 180, 180) sts]

**Rnd 15:** (MC) sc 1, (CC) sc 1, (MC) sc 2, (CC) sc 7, (MC) sc 2, (CC) sc 1, (MC) sc 2 (3, 4, 3), inc x (x, x, 1), repeat from * 9 more times, join with sl st to ch 1 at beginning of rnd. [160 (170, 180, 190) sts]

**Rnd 16** (Last increase rnd for size L): (MC) sc 3, (CC) sc 4, (MC) sc 1, (CC) sc 4, (MC) sc 4 (5, 6, 6), inc x (x, x, 1), repeat from * 9 more times, join with sl st to ch 1 at beginning of rnd. [160 (170, 180, 200) sts]

**Rnd 17:** (MC) sc 5, (CC) sc 2, (MC) sc 1, (CC) sc 2, (MC) sc 6 (7, 8, 10), repeat from * 9 more times, join with sl st to ch 1 at beginning of rnd. [160 (170, 180, 200) sts]

**Rnd 18:** (MC) sc 6, (CC) sc 1, (MC) sc 1, (CC) sc 1, (MC) sc 7 (8, 9, 10), repeat from * 9 more times, join with sl st to ch 1 at beginning of rnd. [160 (170, 180, 200) sts]

Fasten off CC, and skip to armhole join round.

## Yoke Sizes XL to 5XL

**Rnd 1:** Starting with MC, FSC 71. Join the first and last FSC together with a sl st. The first FSC will no longer count as a st.

Work all sts from this point forward in the blo, which helps offset slanting in the colorwork. The ch 1 at the beginning of each rnd does not count as a st. Each rnd corresponds with the same numbered row on the chart.

**Rnd 2 (chart row 2):** (MC) ch 1, sc around, join with a sl st to ch 2 at beginning of rnd. [70 sts]

**Rnd 3:** (CC) ch 1, *sc 6, inc 1, repeat from * 9 more times, join with sl st to ch 1 at beginning of rnd. [80 sts]

**Rnd 4:** (CC) ch 1, * sc 2, (MC) sc 2, (CC) sc 2, (MC) sc 1, inc 1, repeat from * 9 more times, join with sl st to ch 1 at beginning of rnd. [90 sts]

**Rnd 5:** (MC) ch 1, *sc 1, (CC) sc 4, (MC) sc 3, inc 1, repeat from * 9 more times, join with sl st to ch 1 at beginning of rnd. [100 sts]

**Rnd 6:** (MC) ch 1, *sc 2, (CC) sc 2, (MC) sc 5, inc 1, repeat from * 9 more times, join with sl st to ch 1 at beginning of rnd. [110 sts]

**Rnd 7:** (MC) ch 1, *sc 10, inc 1, repeat from * 9 more times, join with sl st to ch 1 at beginning of rnd. [120 sts]

**Rnd 8:** (MC) ch 1, *sc 2, (CC) sc 1, (MC) sc 3, (CC) sc 1, (MC) sc 3, (CC) sc 1, (MC) inc 1, repeat from * 9 more times, join with sl st to ch 1 at beginning of rnd. [130 sts]

**Rnd 9:** (MC) ch 1, *sc 1, (CC) sc 3, (MC) sc 1, (CC) sc 3, (MC) sc 1, (CC) sc 3, (MC) inc 1, repeat from * 9 more times, join with sl st to ch 1 at beginning of rnd. [140 sts]

**Rnd 10:** (MC) ch 1, *sc 2, (CC) sc 1, (MC) sc 3, (CC) sc 1, (MC) sc 3, (CC) sc 1, (MC) sc 2, inc 1, repeat from * 9 more times, join with sl st to ch 1 at beginning of rnd. [150 sts]

**Rnd 11:** (MC) ch 1, *sc 14, inc 1, repeat from * 9 more times, join with sl st to ch 1 at beginning of rnd. [160 sts]

**Rnd 12:** (MC) ch 1, *sc 8, (CC) sc 1, (MC) sc 1, (CC) sc 1, (MC) sc 4, inc 1, repeat from * 9 more times, join with sl st to ch 1 at beginning of rnd. [170 sts]

**Rnd 13:** (MC) ch 1, *sc 7, (CC) sc 2, (MC) sc 1, (CC) sc 2, (MC) sc 4, inc 1, repeat from * 9 more times, join with sl st to ch 1 at beginning of rnd. [180 sts]

**Rnd 14:** (MC) ch 1, *sc 5, (CC) sc 4, (MC) sc 1, (CC) sc 4, (MC) sc 3, inc 1, repeat from * 9 more times, join with sl st to ch 1 at beginning of rnd. [190 sts]

**Rnd 15:** (MC) ch 1, *sc 1, (CC) sc 1, (MC) sc 4, (CC) sc 7, (MC) sc 4, (CC) sc 1, (MC) inc 1, repeat from * 9 more times, join with sl st to ch 1 at beginning of rnd. [200 sts]

**Rnd 16:** (CC) ch 1, *sc 3, (MC) sc 1, (CC) sc 1, (MC) sc 3, (CC) sc 3, (MC) sc 3, (CC) sc 1, (MC) sc 1, (CC) sc 3, (MC) inc 1, repeat from * 9 more times, join with sl st to ch 1 at beginning of rnd. [210 sts]

**Rnd 17** (Last increase rnd for size XL): (MC) ch 1, *sc 1, (CC) sc 1, (MC) sc 4, (CC) sc 7, (MC) sc 4, (CC) sc 1, (MC) sc 2, inc, repeat from * 9 more times, join with sl st to ch 1 at beginning of rnd. [220 sts]

From this point on, size XL will no longer be doing an increase at the end of each part of colorwork. Where the increase normally is, there will be an x, followed by the increases for the other sizes. When a size stops increasing, there will be an x to replace the inc. No matter what size you are making, you will keep doing the following rnds to complete the yoke.

**Rnd 18** (Last increase rnd for size 2XL): (MC) ch 1, *sc 5, (CC) sc 4, (MC) sc 1, (CC) sc 4, (MC) sc 8 (7, 7, 7, 7), inc x (1, 1, 1, 1), repeat from * 9 more times, join with sl st to ch 1 at beginning of rnd. [220 (230, 230, 230, 230) sts]

# Falling Snowflakes Sweater (Continued)

**Rnd 19:** (MC) ch 1, *sc 7, (CC) sc 2, (MC) sc 1, (CC) sc 2, (MC) sc 10 (11, 10, 10, 10), inc x (x, 1, 1, 1), repeat from * 9 more times, join with sl st to ch 1 at beginning of rnd. [220 (230, 240, 240, 240) sts]

**Rnd 20** (Last increase rnd for size 3XL): (MC) ch 1, *sc 8, (CC) sc 1, (MC) sc 1, (CC) sc 1, (MC) sc 11 (12, 12, 12, 12), inc x (x, 1, 1, 1), repeat from * 9 more times, join with sl st to ch 1 at beginning of rnd. [220 (230, 250, 250, 250 sts)]

For the next 3 rounds, follow the instructions for your chosen size.

### Sizes XL and 3XL:

**Rnd 21:** (MC) ch 1, sc around, join with a sl st to ch 1 at beginning of rnd. [220 (230, 250) sts]

**Rnd 22:** (CC) ch 1, sc around, join with a sl st to ch 1 at beginning of rnd. [220 (230, 250) sts]

**Rnd 23:** (MC) ch 1, sc around, join with a sl st to ch 1 at beginning of rnd. [220 (230, 250) sts]

### Sizes 4XL and 5XL:

**Rnd 21** (Last increase rnd for size 4XL): (MC) *sc 24, inc, repeat from * 9 more times, join with sl st to ch 1 at beginning of rnd. [260 sts]

Fasten off the CC, and continue with the MC.

### Size 5XL:

**Rnd 22** (Last increase rnd for size 5XL): (CC) ch 1, *sc 25, inc, repeat from * 9 more times, join with sl st to ch 1 at beginning of rnd. [260 (270) sts]

**Rnd 23:** (MC) ch 1, sc around, join with a sl st to ch 1 at beginning of rnd.

Once you have finished rnd 23, skip to the armhole join rnd for all sizes.

## Armhole Join Round for All Sizes

This next round is a continuation of the yoke, where we will create the armholes to begin crocheting the body. You will start the round like you normally do, and then will be skipping stitches and adding chains to create armholes. For the rest of the pattern, you will only use the MC. Continue doing each rnd in the blo.

**Rnd 1:** (See photo above) ch 1, sc 22 (23, 25, 28, 32, 35, 37, 40, 41), ch 5 (8, 10, 9, 11, 15, 12, 15, 18), sk 35 (38, 40, 44, 46, 50, 52, 50, 53), sc 45 (47, 50, 56, 64, 60, 73, 80, 82), ch 5 (8, 10, 9, 11, 15, 12, 15, 18), sk 35 (38, 40, 44, 46, 50, 52, 50, 53), sc 23 (24, 25, 28, 32, 35, 36, 40, 41), join with sl st to ch 1 at beginning of rnd. [100 (110, 120, 130, 150, 150, 170, 190, 200) sts]

## Body for All Sizes

To crochet the body of the sweater, we will be continuing from the armhole join rnd. The rest of the sweater continues in the round with no colorwork, but still is worked in the blo to maintain the textured look.

**Rnd 1:** ch 1, sc around, including each of the ch sts you did to form the armholes, join with sl st to ch 1 at beginning of rnd. [100 (110, 120, 130, 150, 150, 170, 190, 200) sts]

**Rnd 2:** ch 1, *sc 8 (9, 10, 11, 13, 13, 15, 17, 18), dec 1, repeat from * around, join with sl st to ch 1 at beginning of rnd. [90 (100, 110, 120, 140, 140, 160, 180, 190) sts]

**Rnd 3:** ch 1, sc around, join with sl st to ch 1 at beginning of rnd. [90 (100, 110, 120, 140, 140, 160, 180, 190) sts]

**Rnd 4:** ch 1, *sc 7 (8, 9, 10, 12, 12, 14, 16, 17), dec 1, repeat from * around, join with sl st to ch 1 at beginning of rnd. [80 (90, 100, 110, 130, 130, 150, 170, 180) sts]

**Rnd 5:** ch 1, sc around, including each of the ch sts you did to form the armholes, join with sl st to ch 1 at beginning of rnd. [80 (90, 100, 110, 130, 130, 150, 170, 180) sts]

Repeat rnd 5 till your sweater measures the length that you would like it to, approx. 23 (24, 25, 26, 27, 28, 29, 30, 31)" or 58 (61, 64, 66, 69, 71, 74, 76, 79) cm in length.

Once your sweater reaches the desired length, fasten off and weave in the ends.

## Sleeves

Using the MC, begin the sleeve by joining the yarn through one of the ends of the strand of ch stitches that formed the armhole. I usually do mine in the last chain st toward the back of the underarm of the armhole, which helps the join for the sleeve be toward the back.

**Rnd 1:** ch 1, sc 40 (46, 50, 53, 57, 65, 64, 70, 76), join with sl st to ch 1 at beginning of rnd. [40 (46, 50, 53, 57, 65, 64, 70, 76) sts]

**Rnds 2 through 5:** ch 1, sc around, join with sl st to ch 1 at beginning of rnd. [40 (46, 50, 53, 57, 65, 64, 70, 76) sts]

**Rnd 6:** ch 1, *sc 6 (7, 8, 8, 9, 11, 10, 12, 13), dec 1, repeat from * 4 more times, sc x (1, x, 3, 2, x, 4, x, 1), join with sl st to ch 1 at beginning of rnd. [35 (41, 45, 48, 52, 60, 59, 65, 71) sts]

**Rnds 7 through 11:** ch 1, sc around, join with sl st to ch 1 at beginning of rnd. [35 (41, 45, 48, 52, 60, 59, 65, 71) sts]

**Rnd 12:** ch 1, *sc 5 (6, 7, 7, 8, 10, 9, 11, 12), dec 1, repeat from * 4 more times, sc x (1, x, 3, 2, x, 4, x, 1), join with sl st to ch 1 at beginning of rnd. [30 (36, 40, 43, 47, 55, 54, 60, 66) sts]

**Rnds 13 through 17:** ch 1, sc around, join with sl st to ch 1 at beginning of rnd. [30 (36, 40, 43, 47, 55, 54, 60, 66) sts]

**Rnd 18:** ch 1, *sc 4 (5, 6, 6, 7, 9, 8, 10, 11), dec 1, repeat from * 4 more times, sc x (1, x, 3, 2, x, 4, x, 1), join with sl st to ch 1 at beginning of rnd. [25 (31, 35, 38, 42, 50, 49, 55, 61) sts]

**Rnds 19 through 23:** ch 1, sc around, join with sl st to ch 1 at beginning of rnd. [25 (31, 35, 38, 42, 50, 49, 55, 61) sts]

**Rnd 24:** ch 1, *sc 3 (4, 5, 5, 6, 8, 7, 9, 10), dec 1, repeat from * 4 more times, sc x (1, x, 3, 2, x, 4, x, 1), join with sl st to ch 1 at beginning of rnd. [20 (26, 30, 33, 37, 45, 44, 50, 56) sts]

**Rnds 25 though 29:** ch 1, sc around, join with sl st to ch 1 at beginning of rnd. [20 (26, 30, 33, 37, 45, 44, 50, 56) sts]

**Rnd 30:** ch 1, *sc 2 (3, 4, 4, 5, 7, 6, 8, 9), dec 1, repeat from * 4 more times, sc x (1, x, 3, 2, x, 4, x, 1), join with sl st to ch 1 at beginning of rnd. [15 (21, 25, 28, 32, 40, 39, 45, 51) sts]

**Rnd 31:** ch 1, sc around, join with sl st to ch 1 at beginning of rnd. [15 (21, 25, 28, 32, 40, 39, 45, 51) sts]

Repeat rnd 31 until till your sleeves reach the desired length, approximately 16 (17, 17, 18, 18, 18, 18, 19, 19)" or 41 (43, 43, 46, 46, 46, 46, 48, 48) cm in length.

Fasten off, weave in ends, repeat for other sleeve.

# Charts

## XS-L

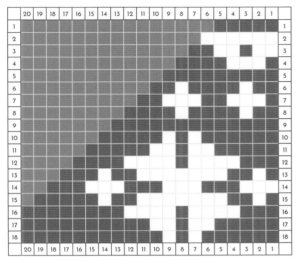

■ Main Color

□ Contrast Color

■ No Stitch

For chart notes and how to read a chart, see pages 15–17.

## XL-5XL

*The Forest Walk Sweater was inspired by walks through the forest during fall or winter, full of crisp mountain air, the smell of pine trees and pine needles crunching under your feet. This sweater design will help teach you how to combine the fair isle technique and waistcoat stitch in the round. It is a top-down circular yoke design that features pine trees and pine cones on the yoke. The pattern is very similar to the Falling Snowflakes Sweater (page 137), with both being made in one piece. You'll stay nice and cozy during the cold months with this sweater.*

# Forest Walk Sweater

## Pattern Level: Advanced

**Gauge:** 4″ x 4″ (10 x 10 cm) square = 11 ws x 16 rnds

**Sizes:** XS (S, M, L, XL, 2X, 3X, 4X, 5X)

**Finished Bust Measurements:**
- 38 (41, 44, 44, 52, 58, 61, 61, 64)″
- 97 (104, 112, 112, 132, 147, 155, 155, 163) cm

**Finished Arm Length:**
- 16 (17, 17, 18, 18, 18, 18, 19, 19)″
- 41 (43, 43, 46, 46, 46, 46, 48, 48) cm

**Finished Sweater Length:**
- 22 (23, 23, 24, 24, 24, 25, 25, 26)″
- 56 (58, 58, 61, 61, 61, 64, 64, 66) cm

**Hook:** 7mm

**Yarn:** Lion Brand Re-Tweed (Yarn Weight 4 Medium, 202 yds [185 m], 3.5 oz [100 g], 40 percent wool, 40 percent polyester, 20 percent acrylic) in two colors:
- Everglade (MC)
- Slate (CC)

**Approximate Yarn Yardage:**

MC = 1000 (1100, 1250, 1460, 1600, 1820, 1970, 2100, 2300) yds (914 [1006, 1143, 1335, 1463, 1664, 1801, 1920, 2103] m)

CC = 200-250 yds (183-229 m) for sizes XS to L and 300-350 (274-320 m) for sizes XL to 5XL

**Abbreviations:**

ch = chain

st(s) = stitch(es)

sc = single crochet

ws = waistcoat stitch (see pages 112-113 for detailed instructions on how to do this stitch)

rnd = round

sl st = slip stitch

MC = main color

CC = contrast color

sk = skip

inc = increase

dec = decrease

yo = yarn over

## Yoke XS to L

Starting with the MC, ch 57. Join first ch to last ch with a sl st. The first ch will no longer count as a stitch.

From this point forward, you can use the chart (page 157) to help with the colorwork. The written pattern below writes out each part of the chart. Each rnd in the yoke corresponds to the same row number on the chart. Be sure to mark on the chart where your chosen size will end as increasing, which can be found within the written pattern.

**Rnd 1:** (MC) ch 1 (ch 1 at the beginning of the rnd does not count as a st throughout the rest of the pattern), sc 56, join with a sl st to ch 1 at beginning of rnd. [56 sts]

**Rnd 2:** (MC) ch 1, ws around, on last ws switch to CC on the last yo of the st, join with a sl st to ch 1 at beginning of rnd. [56 sts]

For the next rnd, you won't use the MC; instead you'll leave it at the rnd join and switch to it at the end of the next rnd.

**Rnd 3:** (CC) ch 1, *ws 6, inc 1, repeat from * around, on last ws switch to MC on the last yo of the st, join with a sl st to ch 1 at beginning of rnd. [64 sts]

We'll now use both the MC and the CC.

**Rnd 4:** (MC) ch 1, *ws 1, (CC) ws 1, (MC) ws 1, (CC) ws 1, (MC) ws 1, (CC) ws 1, (MC) ws 1, (CC) ws 1, repeat from * around, join with a sl st to ch 1 at beginning of rnd. [64 sts]

**Rnd 5:** (MC) ch 1, *ws 2, (CC) ws 1, (MC) ws 3, (CC) ws 1, (MC) inc 1, repeat from * around, join with a sl st to ch 1 at beginning of rnd. [72 sts]

**Rnd 6:** (MC) ch 1, *ws 1, (CC) ws 1, (MC) ws 1, (CC) ws 1, (MC) ws 1, (CC) ws 1, (MC) ws 1, (CC) ws 1, (MC) ws 1, repeat from * around, join with a sl st to ch 1 at beginning of rnd. [72 sts]

**Rnd 7:** (CC) ch 1, *ws 8, inc 1, repeat from * around, join with a sl st to ch 1 at beginning of rnd. [80 sts]

**Rnd 8:** (MC) ch 1, ws around, join with a sl st to ch 1 at beginning of rnd. [80 sts]

**Rnd 9:** (MC) ch 1, *ws 5, (CC) ws 1, (MC) ws 3, inc 1, repeat from * around, join with sl st to ch 1 at beginning of rnd. [88 sts]

**Rnd 10:** (MC) ch 1, *ws 4, (CC) ws 3, (MC) ws 4, repeat from * around, join with sl st to ch 1 at beginning of rnd. [88 sts]

**Rnd 11:** (MC) ch 1, *ws 3, (CC) ws 1, (MC) ws 1, (CC) ws 1, (MC) ws 1, (CC) ws 1, (MC) ws 2, inc 1, repeat from * around, join with sl st to ch 1 at beginning of rnd. [96 sts]

**Rnd 12:** (MC) ch 1, *ws 5, (CC) ws 1, (MC) ws 6, repeat from * around, join with sl st to ch 1 at beginning of rnd. [96 sts]

**Rnd 13:** (MC) ch 1, *ws 4, (CC) ws 3, (MC) ws 4, in next st [(CC) ws 1, (MC) ws 1], repeat from * around, join with sl st to ch 1 at beginning of rnd. [104 sts]

**Rnd 14:** (MC) ch 1, *ws 3, (CC) ws 5, (MC) ws 2, (CC) ws 3, repeat from * around, join with sl st to ch 1 at beginning of rnd. [104 sts]

**Rnd 15:** (MC) ch 1, *ws 2, (CC) ws 1, (MC) ws 2, (CC) ws 1, (MC) ws 2, (CC) ws 1, (MC) ws 2, (CC) ws 1, (MC) inc, repeat from * around, join with sl st to ch 1 at beginning of rnd. [112 sts]

**Rnd 16:** (MC) ch 1, *ws 4, (CC) ws 3, (MC) ws 7, repeat from * around, join with sl st to ch 1 at beginning of rnd. [112 sts]

**Rnd 17:** (MC) ch 1, *ws 3, (CC) ws 5, (MC) ws 5, inc, repeat from * around, join with sl st to ch 1 at beginning of rnd. [120 sts]

**Rnd 18:** (MC) ch 1, *ws 2, (CC) ws 2, (MC) ws 1, (CC) ws 1, (MC) ws 1, (CC) ws 2, (MC) ws 6, repeat from * around, join with sl st to ch 1 at beginning of rnd. [120 sts]

**Rnd 19:** (MC) ch 1, *ws 5, (CC) ws 1, (MC) ws 8, inc, repeat from * around, join with sl st to ch 1 at beginning of rnd. [128 sts]

**Rnd 20:** (MC) ch 1, ws around, join with sl st to ch 1 at beginning of rnd. [128 sts]

**Rnd 21:** (CC) ch 1, *ws 15, inc, repeat from * around, join with sl st to ch 1 at beginning of rnd. [136 sts]

**Rnd 22:** (MC) ch 1, *ws 3, (CC) ws 1, (MC) ws 1, (CC) ws 2, (MC) ws 2, (CC) ws 1, (MC) ws 2, (CC) ws 2, (MC) ws 1, (CC) ws 1, (MC) ws 1, repeat from * around, join with sl st to ch 1 at beginning of rnd. [136 sts]

**Rnd 23:** (MC) ch 1, *ws 2, (CC) ws 1, (MC) ws 3, (CC) ws 2, (MC) ws 3, (CC) ws 2, (MC) ws 3, in next st [(CC) ws 1, (MC) ws 1] (see photos 1 and 2), repeat from * around, join with sl st to ch 1 at beginning of rnd. [144 sts]

**Rnd 24:** (MC) ch 1, *ws 1, (CC) ws 1, (MC) ws 2, (CC) ws 1, (MC) ws 2, (CC) ws 2, (MC) ws 1, (CC) ws 2, (MC) ws 2, (CC) ws 1, (MC) ws 2, (CC) ws 1, repeat from * around, join with sl st to ch 1 at beginning of rnd. [144 sts]

**Rnd 25** (Last increase rnd for size XS): (CC) ch 1, *ws 1, (MC) ws 2, (CC) ws 3, (MC) ws 2, (CC) ws 3, (MC) ws 2, (CC) ws 3, (MC) ws 1, in next stitch [ws 1, (CC) ws 1], repeat from * around, join with sl st to ch 1 at beginning of rnd. [152 sts]

From this point on, size XS will no longer be doing an increase at the end of the colorwork section. Where the increase normally is within the written pattern, there will be an x, followed by the increases for the other sizes. When a size stops increasing, there will be an x to replace the inc. No matter what size you are making, you will keep doing the following rnds to complete the yoke. The colorwork before the increase will have the correct number of ws that you work for your chosen size.

**Rnd 26:** (MC) ch 1, *ws 2, (CC) ws 1, (MC) ws 1, (CC) ws 1, (MC) ws 1, (CC) ws 1, (MC) ws 2, (CC) ws 1, (MC) ws 2, (CC) ws 1, (MC) ws 1, (CC) ws 1, (MC) ws 1, (CC) ws 1, (MC) ws 2, repeat from * around, join with sl st to ch 1 at beginning of rnd. [152 sts]

**Rnd 27** (Last increase rnd for size S): (MC) ch 1, *ws 1, (CC) ws 1, (MC) ws 1, (CC) ws 3, (MC) ws 1, (CC) ws 1, (MC) ws 3, (CC) ws 1, (MC) ws 1, (CC) ws 3, (MC) ws 1, (CC) ws 1, (MC) ws 1 (x, x, x), inc x (1, 1, 1), repeat from * around, join with sl st to ch 1 at beginning of rnd. [152 (160, 160, 160) sts]

# Forest Walk Sweater (Continued)

**Rnd 28:** (MC) ch 1, *ws 2, (CC) ws 1, (MC) ws 1, (CC) ws 1, (MC) ws 1, (CC) ws 1, (MC) ws 5, (CC) ws 1, (MC) ws 1, (CC) ws 1, (MC) ws 1, (CC) ws 1, (MC) ws 2 (3, 3, 3), repeat from * around, join with sl st to ch 1 at beginning of rnd. [152 (160, 160, 160) sts]

**Rnd 29** (Last increase rnd for size M): (MC) ch 1, *ws 1, (CC) ws 1, (MC) ws 1, (CC) ws 3, (MC) ws 1, (CC) ws 1, (MC) ws 3, (CC) ws 1, (MC) ws 1, (CC) ws 3, (MC) ws 1, (CC) ws 1, (MC) ws 1 (2, 1, 1), inc x (x, 1, 1), repeat from * around, join with sl st to ch 1 at beginning of rnd. [152 (160, 168, 168) sts]

**Rnd 30:** (MC) ch 1, *ws 2, (CC) ws 5, (MC) ws 5, (CC) ws 5, (MC) ws 2 (3, 4, 4), repeat from * around, join with sl st to ch 1 at beginning of rnd. [152 (160, 168, 168) sts]

**Rnd 31** (Last increase rnd for size L): (MC) ch 1, *ws 4, (CC) ws 1, (MC) ws 9, (CC) ws 1, (MC) ws 4 (5, 6, 5), inc x (x, x, 1), repeat from * around, join with sl st to ch 1 at beginning of rnd. [152 (160, 168, 176) sts]

Fasten off the CC, and continue using the MC only for the rest of the sweater.

**Rnd 32:** (MC) ch 1, ws around, join with sl st to ch 1 at beginning of rnd. [152 (160, 168, 176) sts]

## Yoke XL to 5XL

Starting with the MC, ch 73. Join first ch to last ch with a sl st. The first ch will no longer count as a stitch.

From this point forward, you can use the chart. Each rnd in the yoke corresponds to the same rnd number on the chart. Be sure to mark on the chart where your chosen size will end increasing, which can be found within the written pattern.

**Rnd 1:** (MC) ch 1, sc 72, join with sl st to the ch 1 at beginning of rnd. [72 sts]

**Rnd 2:** (MC) ch 1, ws around, join with sl st to the ch 1 at beginning of rnd. [72 sts]

**Rnd 3:** (CC) ch 1, *ws 8, inc, repeat from * around, join with sl st to ch 1 at beginning of rnd. [80 sts]

**Rnd 4:** (MC) ch 1, *ws 1, (CC) ws 1, (MC) ws 1, (CC) ws 1, (MC) ws 2, (CC) ws 1, (MC) ws 1, (CC) ws 1, (MC) ws 1, repeat from * around, join with sl st to ch 1 at beginning of rnd. [80 sts]

**Rnd 5:** (MC) ch 1, *ws 2, (CC) ws 1, (MC) ws 4, (CC) ws 1, (MC) ws 1, inc 1, repeat from * around, join with sl st to ch 1 at beginning of rnd. [88 sts]

**Rnd 6:** (MC) ch 1, *ws 1, (CC) ws 1, (MC) ws 1, (CC) ws 1, (MC) ws 2, (CC) ws 1, (MC) ws 1, (CC) ws 1, (MC) ws 2, repeat from * around, join with sl st to ch 1 at beginning of rnd. [88 sts]

**Rnd 7:** (CC) ch 1, *ws 10, inc, repeat from * around, join with sl st to ch 1 at beginning of rnd. [96 sts]

**Rnd 8:** (MC) ch 1, ws around, join with sl st to ch 1 at beginning of rnd. [96 sts]

**Rnd 9:** (MC) ch 1, *ws 11, inc, repeat from * around, join with sl st to ch 1 at beginning of rnd. [104 sts]

**Rnd 10:** (MC) ch 1, *ws 5, (CC) ws 1, (MC) ws 7, repeat from * around, join with sl st to ch 1 at beginning of rnd. [104 sts]

**Rnd 11:** (MC) ch 1, *ws 4, (CC) ws 3, (MC) ws 5, inc, repeat from * around, join with sl st to ch 1 at beginning of rnd. [112 sts]

**Rnd 12:** (MC) ch 1, *ws 3, (CC) ws 5, (MC) ws 6, repeat from * around, join with sl st to ch 1 at beginning of rnd. [112 sts]

**Rnd 13:** (MC) ch 1, *ws 2, (CC) ws 2, (MC) ws 1, (CC) ws 1, (MC) ws 1, (CC) ws 2, (MC) ws 4, inc, repeat from * around, join with sl st to ch 1 at beginning of rnd. [120 sts]

**Rnd 14:** (MC) ch 1, *ws 5, (CC) ws 1, (MC) ws 9, repeat from * around, join with sl st to ch 1 at beginning of rnd. [120 sts]

**Rnd 15:** (MC) ch 1, *ws 3, (CC) ws 5, (MC) ws 5, (CC) ws 1, (MC) inc, repeat from * around, join with sl st to ch 1 at beginning of rnd. [128 sts]

**Rnd 16:** (MC) ch 1, *ws 2, (CC) ws 7, (MC) ws 3, (CC) ws 3, (MC) ws 1, repeat from * around, join with sl st to ch 1 at beginning of rnd. [128 sts]

**Rnd 17:** (MC) ch 1, *ws 1, (CC) ws 2, (MC) ws 2, (CC) ws 1, (MC) ws 2, (CC) ws 2, (MC) ws 3, (CC) ws 1, (MC) ws 1, inc, repeat from * around, join with sl st to ch 1 at beginning of rnd. [136 sts]

**Rnd 18:** (MC) ch 1, *ws 4, (CC) ws 3, (MC) ws 10, repeat from * around, join with sl st to ch 1 at beginning of rnd. [136 sts]

**Rnd 19:** (MC) ch 1, *ws 2, (CC) ws 7, (MC) ws 7, inc, repeat from * around, join with sl st to ch 1 at beginning of rnd. [144 sts]

# Forest Walk Sweater (Continued)

**Rnd 20:** (MC) ch 1, *ws 1, (CC) ws 3, (MC) ws 1, (CC) ws 1, (MC) ws 1, (CC) ws 3, (MC) ws 8, repeat from * around, join with sl st to ch 1 at beginning of rnd. [144 sts]

**Rnd 21:** (MC) ch 1, *ws 5, (CC) ws 1, (MC) ws 11, inc, repeat from * around, join with sl st to ch 1 at beginning of rnd. [152 sts]

**Rnd 22:** (MC) ch 1, ws around, join with sl st to ch 1 at beginning of rnd. [152 sts]

**Rnd 23:** (MC) ch 1, *ws 18, inc, repeat from * around, join with sl st to ch 1 at beginning of rnd. [160 sts]

**Rnd 24:** (CC) ch 1, ws around, join with sl st to ch 1 at beginning of rnd. [160 sts]

**Rnd 25:** (CC) ch 1, *ws 19, inc, repeat from * around, join with sl st to ch 1 at beginning of rnd. [168 sts]

**Rnd 26:** (MC) ch 1, *ws 3, (CC) ws 1, (MC) ws 2, (CC) ws 2, (MC) ws 2, (CC) ws 1, (MC) ws 2, (CC) ws 2, (MC) ws 2, (CC) ws 1, (MC) ws 3, repeat from * around, join with sl st to ch 1 at beginning of rnd. [168 sts]

**Rnd 27:** (MC) ch 1, *ws 2, (CC) ws 1, (MC) ws 4, (CC) ws 2, (MC) ws 3, (CC) ws 2, (MC) ws 4, (CC) ws 1, (MC) ws 1, inc, repeat from * around, join with sl st to ch 1 at beginning of rnd. [176 sts]

**Rnd 28:** (MC) ch 1, *ws 1, (CC) ws 1, (MC) ws 6, (CC) ws 2, (MC) ws 1, (CC) ws 2, (MC) ws 6, (CC) ws 1, (MC) ws 2, repeat from * around, join with sl st to ch 1 at beginning of rnd. [176 sts]

**Rnd 29:** (CC) ch 1, *ws 1, (MC) ws 3, (CC) ws 1, (MC) ws 4, (CC) ws 3, (MC) ws 4, (CC) ws 1, (MC) ws 3, (CC) ws 1, (MC) inc, repeat from * around, join with sl st to ch 1 at beginning of rnd. [184 sts]

**Rnd 30:** (MC) ch 1, *ws 3, (CC) ws 3, (MC) ws 4, (CC) ws 1, (MC) ws 4, (CC) ws 3, (MC) ws 3, (CC) ws 2, repeat from * around, join with sl st to ch 1 at beginning of rnd. [184 sts]

**Rnd 31:** (MC) ch 1, *ws 2, (CC) ws 1, (MC) ws 1, (CC) ws 1, (MC) ws 1, (CC) ws 1, (MC) ws 7, (CC) ws 1, (MC) ws 1, (CC) ws 1, (MC) ws 1, (CC) ws 1, (MC) ws 3, inc, repeat from * around, join with sl st to ch 1 at beginning of rnd. [192 sts]

**Rnd 32:** (MC) ch 1, *ws 1, (CC) ws 1, (MC) ws 1, (CC) ws 3, (MC) ws 1, (CC) ws 1, (MC) ws 5, (CC) ws 1, (MC) ws 1, (CC) ws 3, (MC) ws 1, (CC) ws 1, (MC) ws 4, repeat from * around, join with sl st to ch 1 at beginning of rnd. [192 sts]

**Rnd 33:** (CC) ch 1, *ws 1, (MC) ws 1, (CC) ws 1, (MC) ws 1, (CC) ws 1, (MC) ws 1, (CC) ws 1, (MC) ws 1, (CC) ws 1, (MC) ws 3, (CC) ws 1, (MC) ws 1, (CC) ws 1, (MC) ws 1, (CC) ws 1, (MC) ws 1, (CC) ws 1, (MC) ws 1, (CC) ws 1, (MC) ws 2, inc, repeat from * around, join with sl st to ch 1 at beginning of rnd. [200 sts]

**Rnd 34:** (MC) ch 1, *ws 1, (CC) ws 1, (MC) ws 1, (CC) ws 3, (MC) ws 1, (CC) ws 1, (MC) ws 5, (CC) ws 1, (MC) ws 1, (CC) ws 3, (MC) ws 1, (CC) ws 1, (MC) ws 5, repeat from * around, join with sl st to ch 1 at beginning of rnd. [200 sts]

**Rnd 35** (Last increase rnd for size XL): (CC) ch 1, *ws 1, (MC) ws 1, (CC) ws 5, (MC) ws 1, (CC) ws 1, (MC) ws 3, (CC) ws 1, (MC) ws 1, (CC) ws 5, (MC) ws 1, (CC) ws 1, (MC) ws 3, inc, repeat from * around, join with sl st to ch 1 at beginning of rnd. [208 sts]

From this point on, size XL will no longer be doing an increase at the end of a colorwork section. Where the increase normally is, there will be an x, followed by the increases for the other sizes. When a size stops increasing, there will be an x to replace the inc. No matter what size you are making, you will keep doing the following rnds to complete the yoke. The colorwork before the increase will have the correct number of ws that you work for your chosen size.

**Rnd 36:** (MC) ch 1, *ws 1, (CC) ws 7, (MC) ws 5, (CC) ws 7, (MC) ws 6, repeat from * around, join with sl st to ch 1 at beginning of rnd. [208 sts]

**Rnd 37:** (MC) ch 1, *ws 2, (CC) ws 5, (MC) ws 7, (CC) ws 5, (MC) ws 7 (6, 6, 6), inc x (1, 1, 1, 1) repeat from * around, join with sl st to ch 1 at beginning of rnd. [208 (216, 216, 216, 216) sts]

**Rnd 38:** (MC) ch 1, *ws 4, (CC) ws 1, (MC) ws 11, (CC) ws 1, (MC) ws 9 (10, 10, 10, 10), repeat from * around, join with sl st to ch 1 at beginning of rnd. [208 (216, 216, 216, 216) sts]

Fasten off the CC, and continue using the MC only for the rest of the sweater.

**Size XL:** If the yoke is almost past the bust when worn, skip to the armhole join round. If not, you can continue adding rnds of ws till it reaches the point where it will sit comfortably when you join for the armholes.

**Sizes 2XL to 5XL:** Follow the instructions for your chosen size in the following rnds.

**Rnd 39** (Last increase rnd for size 2XL): (MC) ch 1, *ws 26, inc, repeat from * around, join with sl st to ch 1 at beginning of rnd. [224 sts]

**Size 2XL:** Skip to the armhole join, unless you'd like to have the yoke be longer because it doesn't go over the bust in length.

# Forest Walk Sweater (Continued)

## Sizes 3XL to 5XL only:

**Rnd 40:** (MC) ch 1, ws around, join with sl st to ch 1 at beginning of rnd. [224 sts]

**Rnd 41** (Last increase rnd for size 3XL): (MC) ch 1, *ws 27, inc, repeat from * around, join with sl st to ch 1 at beginning of rnd. [232 sts]

**Size 3XL:** Skip to the armhole join, unless you'd like to have the yoke be longer if it doesn't go over the bust in length.

## Sizes 4XL and 5XL only:

**Rnd 42:** (MC) ch 1, ws around, join with sl st to ch 1 at beginning of rnd. [232 sts]

**Rnd 43** (Last increase rnd for size 4XL): (MC) ch 1, *ws 28, inc, repeat from * around, join with sl st to ch 1 at beginning of rnd. [240 sts]

**Size 4XL:** Continue to the armhole join rnd, unless you'd like to have the yoke be longer if it doesn't go over the bust in length.

## Size 5XL only:

**Rnd 44:** (MC) ch 1, ws around, join with sl st to ch 1 at beginning of rnd. [240 sts]

**Rnd 45:** (MC) ch 1, *ws 29, inc, repeat from * around, join with sl st to ch 1 at beginning of rnd. [248 sts]

**Size 5XL:** Continue to the armhole join rnd, unless you'd like to have the yoke be longer if it doesn't go over the bust in length.

## Armhole Join Round for All Sizes

Before starting the armhole join rnd, I recommend using stitch markers to mark where you will skip stitches. Read the rnd below, count to where you skip and mark that st with a stitch marker. Then count how many stitches you skip, and mark that last st with a stitch marker. Count across to where the next armhole begins, and do the same thing. The rnd below will detail all of the numbers you need.

**Rnd 1:** ch 1, ws 20 (21, 22, 22, 29, 31, 32, 33, 33), ch 11 (14, 16, 16, 14, 18, 20, 19, 22), sk 35 (38, 40, 44, 46, 50, 52, 55, 58) (see photo above), ws 41 (42, 44, 44, 58, 62, 64, 65, 66), ch 11 (14, 16, 16, 14, 18, 20, 19, 22), sk 35 (38, 40, 44, 46, 50, 52, 55, 58), ws 21 (21, 22, 22, 29, 31, 32, 32, 33), join with sl st to ch 1 at beginning of rnd. [104 (112, 120, 120, 144, 160, 168, 168, 176) sts]

## Body for All Sizes

**Rnd 1:** ch 1, ws around, including the ch sts where you will do 1 sc in each ch, join with sl st to ch 1 at beginning of rnd. [104 (112, 120, 120, 144, 160, 168, 168, 176) sts]

**Rnd 2:** ch 1, *ws 11 (12, 13, 13, 16, 18, 19, 19, 20), dec, repeat from * around, join with sl st to ch 1 at beginning of rnd. [96 (104, 112, 112, 136, 152, 160, 160, 168) sts]

**Rnd 3:** ch 1, ws around, join with sl st to ch 1 at beginning of rnd. [96 (104, 112, 112, 136, 152, 160, 160, 168) sts]

**Rnd 4:** ch 1, *ws 10 (11, 12, 12, 15, 17, 18, 18, 19), dec, repeat from * around, join with sl st to ch 1 at beginning of rnd. [88 (96, 104, 104, 128, 144, 152, 152, 160) sts]

**Rnd 5:** ch 1, ws around, join with sl st to ch 1 at beginning of rnd. [88 (96, 104, 104, 128, 144, 152, 152, 160) sts]

**Rnd 6:** ch 1, *ws 9 (10, 11, 11, 14, 16, 17, 17, 18), dec, repeat from * around, join with sl st to ch 1 at beginning of rnd. [80 (88, 96, 96, 120, 136, 144, 144, 152) sts]

**Rnd 7:** ch 1, ws around, join with sl st to ch 1 at beginning of rnd. [80 (88, 96, 96, 120, 136, 144, 144, 152) sts]

**Rnd 8:** ch 1, *ws 8 (9, 10, 10, 13, 15, 16, 16, 17), dec, repeat from * around, join with sl st to ch 1 at beginning of rnd. [72 (80, 88, 88, 112, 128, 136, 136, 144) sts]

**Rnd 9:** ch 1, ws around, join with sl st to ch 1 at beginning of rnd.

For the next fifteen rnds, or until your sweater reaches the waist, repeat rnd 9. Once you've reached the waist, continue with the next rnd.

**Next rnd:** ch 1, *ws 8 (9, 10, 10, 13, 15, 16, 16, 17), inc, repeat from * around, join with sl st to ch 1 at beginning of rnd. [80 (88, 96, 96, 120, 136, 144, 144, 152) sts]

**Next rnd:** ch 1, ws around, join with sl st to ch 1 at beginning of rnd. [80 (88, 96, 96, 120, 136, 144, 144, 152) sts]

**Next rnd:** ch 1, *ws 9 (10, 11, 11, 14, 16, 17, 17, 18), inc, repeat from * around, join with sl st to ch 1 at beginning of rnd. [88 (96, 104, 104, 128, 144, 152, 152, 160) sts]

**Next rnd:** ch 1, ws around, join with sl st to ch 1 at beginning of rnd. [88 (96, 104, 104, 128, 144, 152, 152, 160) sts]

Continue repeating the last rnd until your sweater reaches the desired length, approximately 22 (23, 23, 24, 24, 24, 25, 25, 26)" or 56 (58, 58, 61, 61, 61, 64, 64, 66) cm. That is around 88 (92, 92, 96, 96, 96, 100, 100, 104) rows total.

Fasten off and weave in the ends.

## Sleeves

Using the MC, begin the sleeve by joining the yarn through one of the ends of the strand of ch stitches that formed the armhole.

**Rnd 1:** ch 1, ws 46 (52, 56, 60, 60, 68, 71, 75, 80), join with sl st to ch 1 at beginning of rnd. [46 (52, 56, 60, 60, 68, 71, 75, 80) sts]

**Rnds 2 through 6:** ch 1, ws around join with sl st to ch 1 at beginning of rnd. [46 (52, 56, 60, 60, 68, 71, 75, 80) sts]

**Rnd 7:** ch 1, *ws 7 (8, 9, 10, 10, 11, 12, 13, 14), dec, repeat from * 4 more times, ws 1 (2, 1, x, x, 3, 1, x, x), join with sl st to ch 1 at beginning of rnd. [41 (47, 51, 55, 55, 63, 66, 70, 75) sts]

# Forest Walk Sweater (Continued)

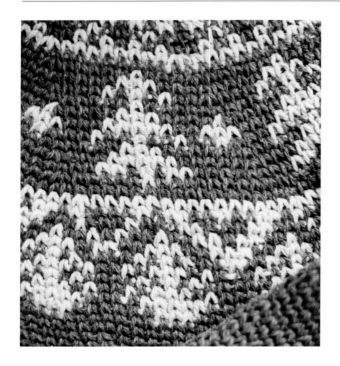

**Rnds 8 through 17:** ch 1, ws around, join with sl st to ch 1 at beginning of rnd. [41 (47, 51, 55, 55, 63, 66, 70, 75) sts]

**Rnd 18:** ch 1, *ws 6 (7, 8, 9, 9, 10, 11, 12, 13), dec, repeat from * 4 more times, ws 1 (2, 1, x, x, 3, 1, x, x), join with sl st to ch 1 at beginning of rnd. [36 (42, 46, 50, 50, 58, 61, 65, 70) sts]

**Rnds 19 through 29:** ch 1, ws around, join with sl st to ch 1 at beginning of rnd. [36 (42, 46, 50, 50, 58, 61, 65, 70) sts]

**Rnd 30:** ch 1, *ws 5 (6, 7, 8, 8, 9, 10, 11, 12), dec, repeat from * 4 more times, ws 1 (2, 1, x, x, 3, 1, x, x), join with sl st to ch 1 at beginning of rnd. [31 (37, 41, 45, 45, 53, 56, 60, 65) sts]

**Rnds 31 through 40:** ch 1, ws around, join with sl st to ch 1 at beginning of rnd. [31 (37, 41, 45, 45, 53, 56, 60, 65) sts]

**Rnd 41:** ch 1, *ws 4 (5, 6, 7, 7, 8, 9, 10, 11), dec, repeat from * 4 more times, ws 1 (2, 1, x, x, 3, 1, x, x), join with sl st to ch 1 at beginning of rnd. [26 (32, 36, 40, 40, 48, 51, 55, 60) sts]

**Next rnd:** ch 1, ws around, join with sl st to ch 1 at beginning of rnd. [26 (32, 36, 40, 40, 48, 51, 55, 60) sts]

For the rest of the sleeve, repeat the last rnd until you reach the desired length, approximately 16 (17, 17, 18, 18, 18, 18, 19, 19)″ or 41 (43, 43, 46, 46, 46, 46, 48, 48) cm, which is approximately 64 (68, 68, 72, 72, 72, 72, 76, 76) rows total.

Fasten off and weave in the ends.

# Charts

■ Main Color

□ Contrast Color

■ No Stitch

For chart notes and how to read a chart, see pages 15–17.

## XS–L

## XL–5XL

# Acknowledgments

First off, I want to thank Rebecca, Sarah and the incredible team at Page Street Publishing. Thank you for making my dreams of being an author come true! I never would have thought that at the beginning of a pandemic, a publishing company would take a chance on me and make my dreams a reality. I couldn't have asked for a better team to work with!

These patterns wouldn't be what they are without my incredible tech editor, Emily from Fiat Fiber Arts. Emily, you went above and beyond to make these patterns just right, and I couldn't be more grateful. From checking the charts line by line to printing out pages of patterns and doing endless math, you have helped my patterns be at their best.

A big shoutout to Lion Brand Yarn for providing all of the wonderful and beautiful yarn for this book. Thank you Mark and the Lion Brand team for believing in me and supporting me in this way. It is a dream to get to work with Lion Brand, and I have to pinch myself a bit each day that I get to work with you all.

I would have never gotten to the place I am today without the support of my followers and audience. When I dreamed of starting my blog, I would have never thought it would get to the point where I would be able to write a book. Every like, share, purchase, page view and kind message encourages me to keep pursuing this dream of being a crochet designer. I could have never done it without you all!

Last but not least, I want to thank my husband, Stephen, who has been my biggest cheerleader and encouraged me to follow my dreams. Without you, E'Claire Makery wouldn't be possible, and I wouldn't have taken that first step to launch my crochet blog. You've been with me each step of the way, and thank you for encouraging me to write this book. From making dinner to cleaning our apartment, making sure I got sleep and holding me through the stressful moments, you have been the most incredible husband. I love you and am so glad you are the partner I get to go through life with and see where this crochet journey takes me!

# About the Author

Claire Goodale is the designer and maker behind the crochet blog E'Claire Makery. She has been crocheting since she was seven years old and loves teaching others how to express themselves through crochet colorwork. She works regularly as a designer for Lion Brand Yarn and is a WeCrochet Ambassador. Her work can be found on her blog, www.eclairemakery.com, her Etsy and Ravelry stores and in publications such as *Happily Hooked Magazine*, *Simply Crochet* and *Inside Crochet*. She lives in California with her husband, Stephen, and when she's not crocheting, she is probably reading a book or dreaming about what new pattern she will work on next.

# Index